Family Life Skills

Student Applications Guide

• • •

Second Edition

BJU PRESS

Greenville, South Carolina

This textbook was written by members of the faculty and staff of Bob Jones University. Standing for the "old-time religion" and the absolute authority of the Bible since 1927, Bob Jones University is the world's leading Fundamentalist Christian university. The staff of the University is devoted to educating Christian men and women to be servants of Jesus Christ in all walks of life.

Providing unparalleled academic excellence, Bob Jones University prepares its students through its offering of over one hundred majors, while its fervent spiritual emphasis prepares their minds and hearts for service and devotion to the Lord Jesus Christ.

If you would like more information about the spiritual and academic opportunities available at Bob Jones University, please call **1-800-BJ-AND-ME** (1-800-252-6363). www.bju.edu

Note: The fact that materials produced by other publishers may be referred to in this volume does not constitute an endorsement by BJU Press of the content or theological position of materials produced by such publishers. The position of BJU Press, and of Bob Jones University, is well known. Any references and ancillary materials are listed as an aid to the student or the teacher and in an attempt to maintain the accepted academic standards of the publishing industry.

Family Life Skills
Student Applications Guide
Second Edition

Anna Sumabat Turner, M.Ed.

Editor
Catherine Morris
Compositor
Jennifer Hearing
Project Manager
Victor Ludlum
Design Coordinator
Holly Gilbert
Cover and Title Page
Elly Kalagayan

Photo Acquisition
Susan Perry
Illustrators
Christy Bruckner
Paula Cheadle
Aaron Dickey
MaryAnn Lumm
Dave Schuppert
Lynda Slattery

The following artist is represented by **Wilkinson Studios, LLC:**
Bob Brugger

Photograph Credits
The following agencies and individuals have furnished materials to meet the photographic needs of this textbook. We wish to express our gratitude to them for their important contribution.

Comstock
Getty Images
Hemera Technologies

www.comstock.com 98
Getty Images 1, 8, 9, 14, 26, 29, 35, 38, 49 (both), 50, 51, 58, 60, 62, 65 (all), 97, 125, 133 (all), 143, 145, 146
©2003 Hemera Technologies, Inc., All Rights Reserved 148

Produced in cooperation with the Bob Jones University Family and Consumer Sciences Division of the College of Arts and Science, the School of Religion, and Bob Jones Academy.

Contents

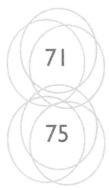

What Is a Family?

CHAPTER 1 • The Family Examined

In the space below, write your definition of the family.

Interview five people of varying ages. Ask them the question *"What is a family?"* In the table below, identify the person, his age, his relationship to you or his occupation, and his response. These comments will be used in the class discussion tomorrow.

	Name	Age	Relationship	Response
1.				
2.				
3.				
4.				
5.				

Read Chapter 1 at this time.
Answer the following questions.

1. What is a nuclear family?

2. What is an extended family?

3. What is the biblical definition of a family?

Genealogical Tree

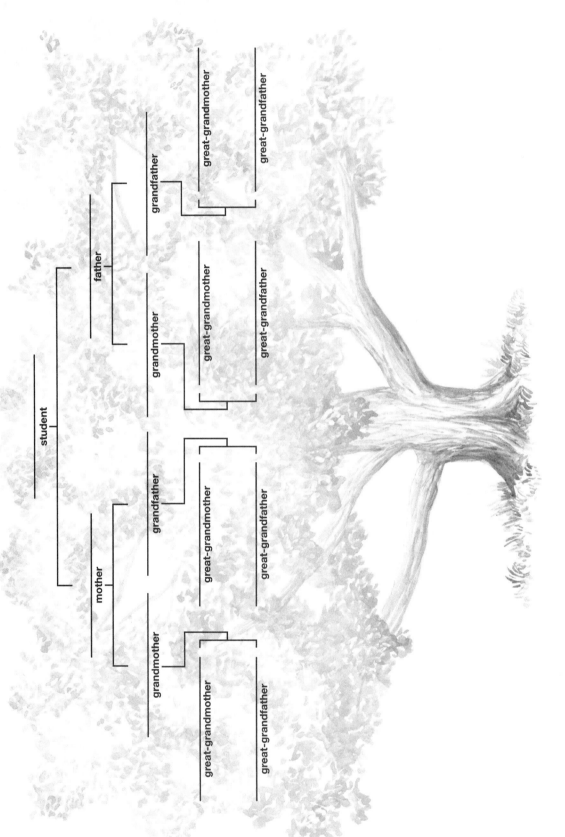

student

father

mother

grandfather

grandmother

grandfather

grandmother

great-grandmother

great-grandfather

great-grandmother

great-grandfather

great-grandmother

great-grandfather

great-grandmother

great-grandfather

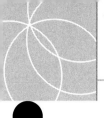

Joseph's Godly Character
CHAPTER 1 • The Family Examined

Joseph exemplified a godly character even in his youth. Read the account of his life in Genesis 37–45. Reread the verses listed below and state in your own words the character qualities Joseph manifested.

Genesis 37:13 _____

Genesis 39:2–4 _____

Genesis 39:6 _____

Genesis 39:12 _____

Genesis 39:20 _____

Genesis 41:14 _____

Genesis 41:16 _____

Genesis 41:39 _____

Genesis 42:18 _____

Genesis 45:5 _____

_____

Genesis 45:11 _____

_____

In what ways can you develop and apply these qualities in your own life and in your relationship with your family?

Project with the Elderly
CHAPTER 1 • The Family Examined

I. General instructions
A. Buy or make a notebook for this project.
B. Correspond with a grandparent, other relative, or friend over sixty years of age at least three times this semester to find out what life was like when he was your age.
- Make a copy of every letter that you send. Put each letter in your notebook.
- Put every letter you receive in your project notebook.
- Hand in the copy of your first letter on _____. Other copies of letters need to be handed in on _____ and the final letter on _____.
- Make sure that your letters are informative. Include school and family news. Your letters should not appear to be written for an assignment. Show love and interest.
- In your first letter, tell about your Family Life Skills class. Explain that everyone is writing to his grandparents to compare their teenage life with teenage life today. Ask if he would be willing to help you with your project.
C. If available, include copies of photographs and pictures in your project notebook.

II. Procedure
A. Select any three of the following topics. If there is another topic that you would like to learn about that is not listed, ask your teacher for approval.
- Child-care practices
- Church and its activities
- Ways teenagers could earn money
- Transportation
- Grocery shopping
- Clothing (everyday, sports clothes, shoes, accessories)
- High-school life (sports, clubs, classes, schedules, friends, lunch, homeroom, lockers, cheerleaders, homework)
- Holiday traditions
- Hobbies, recreation, entertainment
- The kitchen (appliances, setup, uses)
- How Sunday was spent
- Family outings and vacations
- Their engagement, wedding, and beginning of a home
- Dating (where they went, what restrictions and standards were set, at what age they were allowed to date)
B. For each topic chosen, do the following:
1. Write the topic at the top of a page. (You may write or type for this project; just be consistent.)
2. Write what you think your grandparent will say about that topic. If you do not know, then guess. Minimum length is one paragraph.
3. Hand in three pages on _____. Later, put them in your project notebook.
4. Each of the three times you write to your grandparent, ask about one of your topics. You may want to share with him what you think he will say.
5. When your grandparent writes to you about that topic, summarize what he said on the bottom half of the page.

Project with the Elderly, cont.

CHAPTER 1 • The Family Examined

C. Find out what things make your grandparent happiest today.
　　1. On a separate sheet of paper in your project notebook, list five things that you think would make your grandparent happiest today.
　　2. In one of your letters ask him to share with you what five things would make him the happiest.
　　3. At the bottom of the sheet giving your guesses, write what he told you.

D. Find out what advice your grandparent would give to teenagers today if given the opportunity.
　　1. On a separate sheet of paper in your project notebook, list three things that you think your grandparent would advise teenagers.
　　2. In one of your letters, ask him to share his advice with you.
　　3. At the bottom of the sheet giving your guesses, write what he told you.

E. Between the beginning and the completion of this project, do three extra things for your grandparent.
　　1. Examples: make a long-distance phone call (do not reverse the charges); send a picture of yourself, a bookmark, or other small gift; send a card on a holiday or for no special occasion; bake a gift.
　　2. Record each "extra" and the date done on a separate sheet of paper in your project notebook.

F. Other information
　　1. Do the complete assignment with one person. You may, however, supplement your project by writing to other grandparents, relatives, or friends over sixty and asking them questions.
　　2. If your grandparent lives in town, ask him to give you handwritten replies—something you will treasure through the years.
　　3. You may send a cassette tape in place of one of the letters. Write a summary of what each of you said on the tape and include the summaries in place of the letters.
　　4. You may do a video interview with your grandparent. If you do this, write a summary of your conversation in place of the letters.
　　5. You may write to your grandparent on the Internet only if you have a printer and can make a copy of your messages to him and his responses to you.

III. Benefits of this project
A. *You* will benefit in the following ways.
　　1. You will learn many new and interesting things about life two generations ago.
　　2. You will find out things about your grandparent that you and perhaps your parents never knew.
　　3. You will realize how much your interest in your grandparent means to him.
　　4. You will recognize that many of the conflicts common to youth have not changed.
　　5. You will have a short document of your family history.
　　6. You will promote unity in your own family.
B. *Your grandparent* will benefit in the following ways.
　　1. He will get informative letters from a grandchild to add interest to life.
　　2. He will recognize your love and interest in his life: past and present.
　　3. He will be pleased that you as a young person want to learn from him.

Project with the Elderly, cont.

CHAPTER 1 • The Family Examined

IV. Evaluation

A. When you have completed the project, write two evaluations (summaries) of what you learned about your grandparent as a teenager and as an older person now.

   1. Evaluation of the past
- Compare what you guessed his teenage life was like to what he told you. How accurate were your guesses? What surprised you?
- Explain why you would or would not want to live in "the good old days." What did they have that you do not? What do you have that they did not?

   2. Evaluation of the present
- Compare what you guessed would make him the happiest with what he said.
- Compare what you guessed his advice to teens would be with what it actually was.
- Summarize what you learned about your grandparent as an elderly person living today. What are his needs and desires? What can you do to make him happier? Do you feel he enjoyed participating in this project? Explain.

B. The entire project is due _____.

Christian Family Life Cycle

CHAPTER 1 • The Family Examined

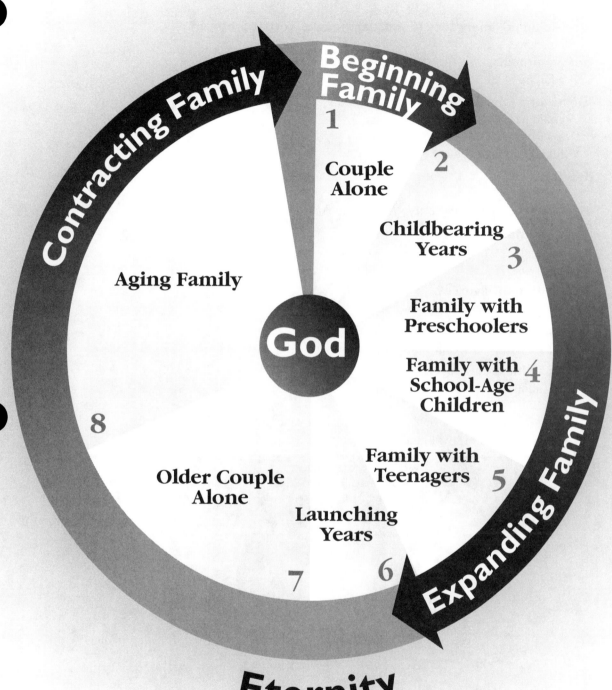

Romans 11:36 "For of him, and through him,
and to him, are all things."

Crisis Times for the Family
CHAPTER 1 • The Family Examined

Catastrophic emergency (flood, earthquake, tornado, bomb)
- insurance
- escape route
- equipment

Death of a family member
- assurance of salvation
- a will
- funeral arrangements

Fire or theft
- insurance
- safety precautions (security systems, smoke detectors, fire extinguishers)

Loss of employment
- savings
- insurance

Separation or divorce*
- strong relationship with God

Serious accident
- insurance (medical and auto)

Serious illness diagnosed
- insurance

*One does not plan for divorce. However, if anyone in the family goes through a divorce, the Lord will guide and strengthen during this crisis.

Crisis Times for the Family, cont.

CHAPTER 1 • The Family Examined

Essential Benefits of the Family

- Love, emotional support, nurture, care, solidarity, and instruction for survival and a satisfying life
- A common bond for members to work together in achieving goals
- A basis of identity for the individual
- A continuation of chosen values passed from generation to generation

How does God give family members an opportunity to help during times of crisis?

Consider one member of your family who took the opportunity to be a special help or spiritual inspiration to you in a family or personal crisis. Write this person a thank-you note, using the space below to write the rough draft. Inform your teacher when the note of appreciation was rewritten and sent.

Family Mission Statement
CHAPTER 2 • Family Unity

Many organizations have a mission statement—a written statement that specifies function and purpose. Unfortunately, families often function without a clear statement of their purpose. Most Christian families just "understand" that they want to serve God. However, in forming a mission statement, the family is forced to communicate, delineate, and commit to specific ideals and actions.

A family mission statement is the written creed or stated philosophy of a family unit. It should clarify what a family believes to be its purpose, its goals, and the major principles for accomplishing those goals.

In this activity, the parents must be the leaders and guides. It is important that every family member contribute to the discussion and formation of the family mission statement. Part of the value of this exercise is based on the creation of the statement; it presents an opportunity for family members to communicate with one another.

You are responsible for taking notes, for making sure that the activity questions are answered, and for neatly writing or typing the final family statement. Once the family mission statement has been graded, your family may consider having it framed and placed in a prominent place in your home to remind the entire family of their mission. Because the family unit is constantly changing, the mission statement should be reviewed and updated at least once a year.

If your parents are unsaved or you are unable to do this project with your family, construct a family mission statement that you would like to incorporate into your future home.

Sample Statements of Business Organizations

Bob Jones University
Within the cultural and academic soil of liberal arts higher education, Bob Jones University exists to grow Christlike character that is Scripturally disciplined; others-serving; God-loving; Christ-proclaiming; and focused above.

Bob Jones University Press
The mission of Bob Jones University Press is to provide excellent products and services that meet the needs of customers, support and extend the ministry of Bob Jones University, and promote the cause of Christ.

These samples are brief yet thorough. The family statement that you and your family construct will be a bit longer and more descriptive.

Family Mission Statement, cont.

CHAPTER 2 • Family Unity

Constructing Your Family's Mission Statement

Before you construct a family mission statement, let your parents discuss the following instructions with each other. Give them time to format a rough draft of what they think. After they have agreed on the major points, discuss the project with the whole family.

Step 1: Begin with a sentence identifying your family's name. Add a foundational statement indicating the sovereignty of God and the way to obtain His guidance. Remember the principles taught in Romans 11:36.

Step 2: Write a statement that clearly defines the purpose and objectives of your family. Why is your family here? What does God want your family to accomplish?

Step 3: State specific clarifications that show how your family should accomplish its objectives. What biblical principles will motivate your family members to focus on the family objectives?

Step 4: Conclude by specifying why it is important to focus on God. What does pleasing and imitating Christ have to do with the family?

Step 5: Read through the mission statement that all of you have constructed. Are any changes needed? Is it clear? Does it state what your family believes, why they believe it, and how they act upon it? Can the basic statement be condensed in any way without sacrificing essential principles or concepts?

Step 6: Neatly write or type your family mission statement. Place it in a folder to protect it from getting wrinkled or dirty. After your teacher has given you credit for completing this project, return the certificate to your parents.

Elements of Family Unity

CHAPTER 2 • Family Unity

1. **Salvation—The proper relationship between each family member and the Lord**
   You can establish a right relationship with God. Do you know Christ as your personal Savior? Have you asked Him to forgive you of your sins? Have you established a time of thorough daily Bible study and prayer? Does your life show the fruit of the Spirit? A proper relationship with the Lord does not imply that you will be perfect or always do the right thing, but it does mean that you will grow in the Lord—next year you should be a more mature Christian than you are now. This element is basic to family unity. Until your relationship with the Lord is right, you will not be able to establish right relationships with other family members.

2. **Relation—Proper role relationships between family members**
   The relationships between family members have a direct influence on the unity of the family. If you and your mother or you and a brother or sister constantly argue, your family will remain divided. Amos 3:3 asks, "Can two walk together, except they be agreed?" Family members have to learn to get along together. I Peter 4:8 explains how to achieve that harmony: "And above all things have fervent charity [love] among yourselves; for charity shall cover the multitude of sins." It is a love for God in the hearts of His children that enables them to love their family members even in trying circumstances.

3. **Communication—Healthy expression among family members**
   Communication involves speech and actions as well as listening. Family members should be honest and open with one another without using this openness as an excuse to be degrading and disrespectful. Ephesians 4:29 admonishes, "Let no corrupt communication proceed out of your mouth, but that which is good to the use of edifying, that it may minister grace unto the hearers." Speech to others in general, and to one's family in particular, should always be uplifting and constructive. Truth should be spoken in love rather than in spite. Rather than "speaking your mind," temper your words with lovingkindness.

4. **Consideration—Respect for other family members and their personal property**
   The basis for this element is Matthew 7:12: "Therefore all things whatsoever ye would that men should do to you, do ye even so to them: for this is the law and the prophets." Do you want your sister to borrow your clothes without asking? Do you want your mother to contradict every opinion you offer? The obvious answer is no, and your biblical response should be to refrain from doing those things to others. No home can be harmonious unless family members respect one another and their property.

5. **Cooperation—Responsibilities shared with one another**
   Galatians 6:2 and 6:5 are explicit on this point: "Bear ye one another's burdens, and so fulfill the law of Christ. . . . For every man shall bear his own burden." In a smoothly run home each person takes care of his own responsibilities and helps with general family responsibilities.

6. **Recreation—Good times and fellowship enjoyed together**
   A thousand obligations can stand in the way of family togetherness. Both teenagers and parents must determine to set aside some time daily and weekly for family talks and outings.

Things of Importance
CHAPTER 2 • Family Unity

Step I

On a separate sheet of paper, make a list of the things you possess that are important to you.

Step II

If you knew that your town and home would be destroyed (by a hurricane, volcano, or flood), what would you take with you as you evacuate? Your family has one pickup truck and one compact car. What things would need to be put into the vehicles? Add to the list if necessary, but place a check by all items that would fit in the vehicles.

Step III

Now that your family is driving away, you are faced with a problem. Your pickup truck gets mired in a ditch. You cannot stay; you are not in a safe place. What must be taken out and transferred to the car? Now, underline those things that you and your family have in your compact car.

Step IV

Of all times to have car trouble! Your car has stopped and will not go any farther. You will have to walk the last five miles and carry your possessions with you. Anything left behind will be destroyed. No one will give you a ride; everyone is fleeing the city. What things are of importance now? Place a circle around those items you can carry or take with you.

Step V

On the back of your sheet of paper, evaluate what you have learned. If you can buy and replace items, are they really important? What did you bring into the world with you when you were born? What can you take with you into heaven?

Lessons Learned

CHAPTER 2 • Family Unity

This activity provides an opportunity for you to talk things over with your parents. If several family members do not like the time selected for family devotions, set a different one.

I. When does your family have family devotional time? Why do you like (or not like) this time of day for family devotions?

II. Use this list for ideas on how to create variety and interest in your family devotional time. Mark all of the following items that are included in your family devotional time.

- One song
- Two songs
- More than two songs
- Bible reading
- Devotional book reading
- Devotional lesson given
- Object lessons

- Testimonies
- Missionary letters
- Prayer led by one person
- Prayer led by more than one person
- Prayer led by each family member
- Other elements: _____

III. Star the three items above that you enjoy the most. Why do you especially enjoy the starred items?

IV. When do you have your personal devotions? What method of Bible study do you use?

V. Complete the following chart by noting daily the lessons you learned during your family devotions. In the second column, note the principles or lessons you learned from your personal devotions.

Day	Family Devotions Lessons Learned	Personal Devotions Lessons Learned
Sunday		
Monday		
Tuesday		
Wednesday		
Thursday		
Friday		
Saturday		

VI. Would you learn more (pay closer attention and remember more) if you had to chart your learning all the time? Would keeping a devotional journal help you get more from your family devotions? Your personal devotions?

Devotional Survey

CHAPTER 2 • Family Unity

1. Find three verses that support the need for Bible study and meditation. Write these verses out completely on another sheet of paper and identify their references.

2. Survey each of your family members.

N →
A
M
E

	NAME				
What is the best time for the family to have devotions together?					
Do you have any suggestions about the devotional book or study?					
What type of framework would you like to have in family devotional time?					
A. One song					
B. Two songs					
C. More than two songs					
D. Bible reading					
E. Devotional book reading					
F. Devotional lesson given					
G. Object lessons					
H. Testimonies					
I. Missionary letters					
J. Prayer led by one person					
K. Prayer led by more than one person					
L. Prayer led by each family member					
M. Other elements: _____					

3. Once the survey has been handed in to your teacher for credit, give your findings and your survey project to your parents. Your parents will be the ones to actually establish the time and activities for family devotions.

Family Traditions

CHAPTER 2 • Family Unity

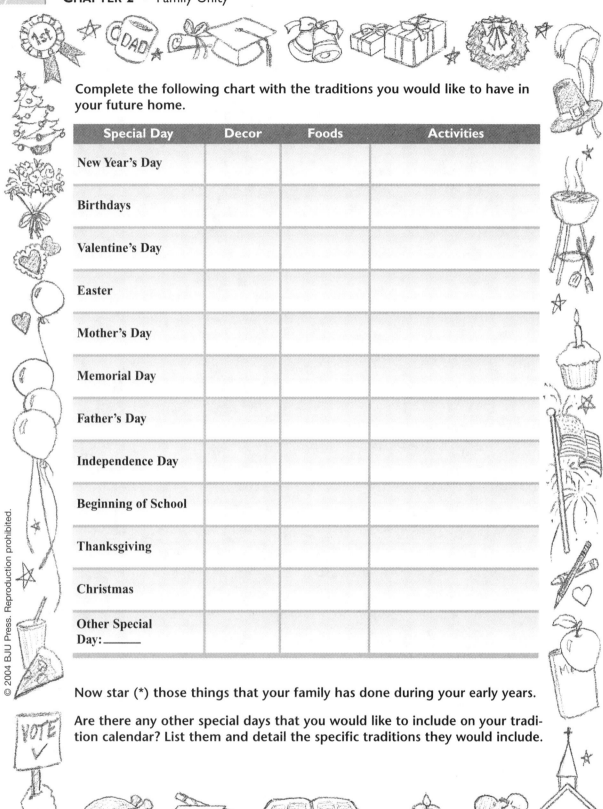

Complete the following chart with the traditions you would like to have in your future home.

Special Day	Decor	Foods	Activities
New Year's Day			
Birthdays			
Valentine's Day			
Easter			
Mother's Day			
Memorial Day			
Father's Day			
Independence Day			
Beginning of School			
Thanksgiving			
Christmas			
Other Special Day:_____			

Now star (*) those things that your family has done during your early years.

Are there any other special days that you would like to include on your tradition calendar? List them and detail the specific traditions they would include.

Tract Track

CHAPTER 3 • Spiritual Growth

Assignment

1. Bring to class three different tracts that present the plan of salvation. You will be given one point for each tract that is different from any other brought to class.

2. Before class, use the following charts to analyze the tracts that you have chosen. Be prepared to present your tracts to the class and to give a review of the positive and negative aspects of each. Be ready to defend your analysis in case another member of the class analyzed the same tract but differs in his opinion of it.

3. When analyzing the inclusion of a sample prayer, determine whether the prayer clearly includes the admission or confession that a person is a sinner, a request that God forgive him, and the ideas that salvation comes only through the shed blood of Christ and that prayer alone does not save.

Analysis (Tract 1)

Title or Name of Tract:

Publisher's Address (Where can you write to get one?):

Evaluate the following qualities as:

1 (poor), 2 (fair), 3 (average), 4 (good), 5 (excellent).

Briefly explain your reasons for giving the tract the rating you gave it.

Qualities	1	2	3	4	5	Reasoning
Ability to get one's attention (x 2)						
Capacity to keep one's attention (x 2)						
Thoroughness of the gospel presentation (x 6)						
Clarity of the gospel presentation (x 4)						
Inclusion of a sample prayer (x 2)						
Direction for spiritual growth and discipleship (x 4)						

Total Score

(Multiply the points given for each quality by the indicated factors.)

_____

Score Evaluation:

Tract Track, cont.

CHAPTER 3 • Spiritual Growth

Suggested Age Limits:

Your Recommendation Summary:

Analysis (Tract 2)

Title or Name of Tract:

Publisher's Address (Where can you write to get one?):

Evaluate the following qualities as:

1 (poor), 2 (fair), 3 (average), 4 (good), 5 (excellent).

Briefly explain your reasons for giving the tract the rating you gave it.

Qualities	I	2	3	4	5	Reasoning
Ability to get one's attention (x 2)						
Capacity to keep one's attention (x 2)						
Thoroughness of the gospel presentation (x 6)						
Clarity of the gospel presentation (x 4)						
Inclusion of a sample prayer (x 2)						
Direction for spiritual growth and discipleship (x 4)						

Total Score

(Multiply the points given for each quality by the indicated factors.)

_____

Score Evaluation:

Suggested Age Limits:

Your Recommendation Summary:

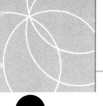

Tract Track, cont.

CHAPTER 3 • Spiritual Growth

Analysis (Tract 3)

Title or Name of Tract:

Publisher's Address (Where can you write to get one?):

Evaluate the following qualities as:

1 (poor), 2 (fair), 3 (average), 4 (good), 5 (excellent).

Briefly explain your reasons for giving the tract the rating you gave it.

Qualities	1	2	3	4	5	Reasoning
Ability to get one's attention (x 2)						
Capacity to keep one's attention (x 2)						
Thoroughness of the gospel presentation (x 6)						
Clarity of the gospel presentation (x 4)						
Inclusion of a sample prayer (x 2)						
Direction for spiritual growth and discipleship (x 4)						

Total Score

(Multiply the points given for each quality by the indicated factors.)

_____

Score Evaluation:

Suggested Age Limits:

Your Recommendation Summary:

Marking the Way

CHAPTER 3 • Spiritual Growth

Making the Map

Do you know how to lead an unsaved person to the Lord? Yes, it is in the Bible, but do you know where to look? For instance, do you know your way down the "Romans Road" well enough to lead a person to Christ?

Match the correct verse (or verses) with each step to salvation. (Some steps have only one verse; some have two.) Then write the verse in the space beside it. Do *not* use your Bible. If you get stuck, you must stop at the point where you need to "repair" your knowledge. Write the word STOP in red ink, close your book, read God's Word, close your Bible, and then continue. If you get stuck again, you must once more write the word STOP in red ink and close your book before you find the correct answers in the Bible.

Romans 3:23   Romans 5:8   Romans 5:12   Romans 6:23   Romans 10:9   Romans 10:13

Acknowledgment

I have sinned.

Penalty

Sin demands God's judgment.

Belief

Jesus, God's Son, died for me.

Acceptance (which involves repentance)

I ask God to forgive me.

1. How many times did you have to stop before you completed the map to salvation?
2. If you had to do this over again, could you accomplish the task without having to repair your knowledge?
3. Now that you know the references and verses, do you not need to use your Bible when leading a person to Christ? Why do you or do you not need to use your Bible?

Marking Your Map

Now that you have successfully mapped the way to salvation using the Romans Road, mark your Bible so that you will have it ready for use.

a. In your Bible, go to the first reference listed above.
b. Underline the verse so that it will be clearly visible to the person you are leading to the Lord.
c. In the margin next to the verse, write the reference for the next verse.
d. Then turn to the next verse, mark it, and write the reference for the next verse beside it.
e. Continue marking the verses in your Bible.

True/False—I have marked each verse of the Romans Road in my Bible.

True/False—I have written in the margin beside each verse the reference for the next verse.

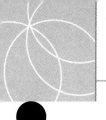

Marking the Way, cont.

CHAPTER 3 • Spiritual Growth

Using Your Map

After you have shown a person what he must do to be saved, encourage him to confess his sin, express his repentance, and ask God for forgiveness in prayer. You may need to help out by starting the prayer. In order to prepare for this, write out what you would pray. You may need to prompt the person, but he should not think that there are certain words that one must pray to be saved.

Continuing on the Road
CHAPTER 3 • Spiritual Growth

If you have been privileged to lead someone to Christ, you have started him on the road toward heaven. The new believer has chosen to walk with Christ toward heaven rather than continue on his own way toward destruction. However, it is much easier to walk on the road with a friend. Jesus is the friend he needs to depend on. He is the friend that is closer than a brother.

A newly saved person needs to grow in the Lord. You have the opportunity and responsibility to guide and encourage the convert. Discipling a new believer is simply teaching him about Christ. After all, how can a person become more like Christ unless he begins to understand more about Him?

Fill in the following outline that could be used in a weekly study to disciple a new believer. Look up both references in your Bible to find each answer.

I. Identity of Christ
A. What the Bible says
1. John 1:1–3 (Colossians 1:16–17) Christ was _____ (He existed before He was born in the flesh).
2. Mark 2:7–11 (Jeremiah 31:34) Only Christ (God) can _____.
3. Matthew 3:17 (II Peter 1:17) "This is _____, in whom I am well pleased."

Note that the following verses show what Christ said or indicated. The corresponding verses in parenthesis are descriptions of God given in the Old Testament. The name for God (Yahweh) was so holy to the Jewish people that His name was not said. They wrote the letters of *YHWH* and used the vowel points for *Adonai* to remind them to say *Adonai*. Jesus clearly claims continuous existence, something only Yahweh can do.

B. What Christ said
1. John 8:58 (Exodus 3:14) "I _____."
2. John 8:12 (Psalm 27:1) "I _____."
3. John 10:11 (Psalm 23:1) "I _____."
4. Matt. 21:14–16 (Ps. 8:2) Christ (Yahweh) has perfected praise "_____ _____."

C. What others said
1. Matthew 14:33 Disciples and those in the ship said, "_____ _____."
2. Matthew 16:16 Peter said, "_____."
3. John 1:1 John said, "_____ _____."
4. John 20:28 Thomas said, "_____."
5. Matthew 27:54 A centurion and others at the crucifixion said, "_____."

Continuing on the Road, cont.
CHAPTER 3 • Spiritual Growth

II. Attributes of Christ (God)

    A. Christ is _____. (I Samuel 2:2 "There is none holy as the Lord: for there is none beside thee: neither is there any rock like our God.")

       1. Christ cannot sin. He hates evil, depravity, and all forms of sin.

       2. Personal Principle: I can do nothing to reconcile myself to a holy God, nor can I live separated from sin without Christ. (The purpose of this principle is to observe how this concept can affect your daily life.)

          a. Because I am redeemed through the blood of Jesus Christ, I must try to live a life that is free from sin. (I Corinthians 6:20 "_____ _____ _____.")

          b. Only through the power of God can I remain separated unto Christ. (I Peter 1:15–16 "But as he which hath called you is holy, so be ye holy in all manner of conversation; Because it is written, _____ _____." Philippians 2:13 "For it is _____ which worketh in you both to will and to do of his good pleasure.")

    B. Christ is _____ (Revelation 1:5 "Unto him that loved us, and washed us from our sins in his own blood.")

       1. Christ wants what is best for me since He loves me.

       2. Personal principle: Jesus will love me in spite of myself.

          a. Nothing can separate me from Christ.

          b. Romans 8:38–39 "For I am persuaded, that neither death, nor life, nor angels, nor principalities, nor powers, nor things present, nor things to come, nor height, nor depth, nor any other creature, _____."

    C. Christ is omniscient. (Psalm 139:1–4 "O Lord, _____ _____.

Thou knowest my downsitting and mine uprising, thou understandest my thought afar off. Thou compassest my path and my lying down, and art acquainted with all my ways. For there is not a word in my tongue, but, lo, O Lord, _____.")

       1. God watches over me in love.

       2. Personal principle:

          _____

          _____

          _____

          _____

          _____

Continuing on the Road, cont.

CHAPTER 3 • Spiritual Growth

D. Christ is omnipresent. (Psalm 139:5–10 "Thou has beset me behind and before and laid thine hand upon me. Such knowledge is too wonderful for me; it is high, I cannot attain unto it. _____ _____ If I ascend up into heaven, thou art there: if I make my bed in hell, behold, thou art there. If I take the wings of the morning and dwell in the uttermost parts of the sea; _____.")

  1. God (Write the reference and the verse.)

    _____

    _____

  2. Personal principle:

    _____

    _____

E. Christ is (Write the reference and the verse.)

  1. Christ

    _____

    _____

  2. Personal principle:

    _____

    _____

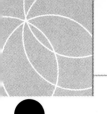

Developing a Biblical Perspective
CHAPTER 3 • Spiritual Growth

Answer the following questions.

What would you change about your physical appearance if you could change it?

What talents do you wish you had?

What circumstances about your life would you change?

Would you change where you live if you could?

Read Ephesians 4:17–32.

What things should be put off?   What things should be put on?
(v. 17) worldliness
(v. 17) former practices
(v. 17) irresponsible behavior
(v. 18) hardness of heart
(v. 19) sinfulness and greed
(v. 22) past lifestyles
(v. 22) corrupt habits
(v. 22) deceitful lusts
(v. 25) lying
(v. 26) anger
(v. 28) stealing
(v. 29) foul language
(v. 30) grieving the Holy Spirit
(v. 31) bitterness
(v. 31) wrath
(v. 31) anger
(v. 31) clamor or noise
(v. 31) evil speaking
(v. 31) malice

Develop a biblical perspective.

List three or more physical characteristics that God gave you that make you special or unique.

List the talents that God has already given you and ways that you can use these talents to serve Him.

List qualities about your parents, siblings, and circumstances that you admire and for which you should be grateful.

List some things in your personal environment for which you should be grateful.

Developing a Biblical Perspective, cont.
CHAPTER 3 • Spiritual Growth

Design plans and goals that would please God.

Look at your answers to the first four questions of this activity and decide whether there is anything that God wants you to change. If you need to improve your personal care or your clothing, write down goals and plans you can implement for improvement. Write down specific changes, goals, and plans that need to be made to develop your talents, improve your circumstances, and correct your environment. Some things cannot be changed. Write out those unchangeable traits and how the Lord would have you to respond. Write out a verse that will enforce the correct heart attitude and include the verse reference.

Appearance

In order to change my _____

I need to _____

_____

Because I cannot change my _____

God would have me to _____

_____

(Verse) _____

_____

_____

Talents

In order to change my _____

I need to _____

_____

Because I cannot change my _____

God would have me to _____

_____

(Verse) _____

_____

_____

Developing a Biblical Perspective, cont.

CHAPTER 3 • Spiritual Growth

Circumstances

In order to change my _____

I need to _____

_____

Because I cannot change my _____

God would have me to _____

_____

(Verse) _____

_____

_____

Environment

In order to change my _____

I need to _____

_____

Because I cannot change my _____

God would have me to _____

_____

(Verse) _____

_____

_____

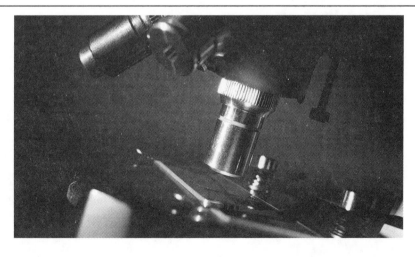

Is the Bible God's Word?

CHAPTER 3 • Spiritual Growth

A Quick Look into a Segment of Christian Apologetics

How many books are in the Old Testament?

How many books are in the New Testament?

How many books are in the Bible?

How many years did it take for all the books in the Bible to be written?
How many authors wrote the Bible?

Were the Bible authors of the same occupation?

Were the Bible authors writing from the same place?

How many generations did the writing of the Bible span?

Which languages were used?

Only the omniscient God could bring unity to so many books written by so many men over such a long period of time.

Only the omnipotent God could preserve His Word over the centuries so that its powerful message can still cut into the human soul and change lives.

BJU Food Pyramid
CHAPTER 4 • Physical Growth

Fats, Oils, & Sweets
use sparingly

Meat, Poultry,
Fish, Dry Beans,
Eggs, & Nuts
2 servings

Milk, Yogurt,
& Cheese
3–4 servings

Fruits
2–4 servings

Vegetables
3–5 servings

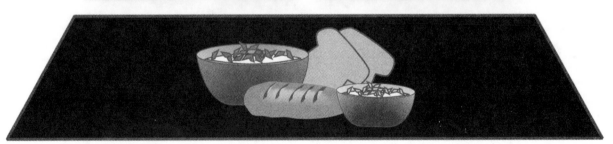

Bread, Cereal, Rice, & Pasta—**6 or more servings**

Eating Analysis
CHAPTER 4 • Physical Growth

For the next seven days, list everything you eat in the spaces below. List specific amounts such as 1/2 c. Cheerios, 1/4 c. milk, 1 tsp. sugar, etc. Underline your daily source of Vitamin C and circle your source (every other day) of Vitamin A. Include all water and beverage intake.

Day	Breakfast	Lunch	Dinner	Snacks
Sunday				
Monday				
Tuesday				
Wednesday				
Thursday				
Friday				
Saturday				

Did you consume a source of Vitamin C daily?
Did you consume a source of Vitamin A every other day?

List the number of servings from each of the food groups on the Food Pyramid that you ate each day. Write "YES" in the "Balanced?" column if your diet was balanced, and "NO" if it was not.

Meat	Milk	Fruit	Vegetable	Grain	Balanced?	Water

Evaluation and comments on your diet for the week:

© 2004 BJU Press. Reproduction prohibited.

32   FAMILY LIFE SKILLS APPLICATIONS GUIDE

Nutrition Helps

Name _____

B Vitamins
Thiamin (B_1)
Riboflavin (B_2)
Niacin (B_3)
Biotin
Pantothenic Acid
B_6 (pyridoxine, pyridoxal, pyridoxamine)
Folate
B_{12} (cobalamin, methylcobalamin, deoxyadenosylcobalamin)

Minerals		
Macrominerals include		*Microminerals needed include*

Macrominerals include		*Microminerals needed include*	
Calcium	Potassium	Iron	Fluoride
Phosphorus	Sodium	Iodine	Cobalt
Magnesium	Chloride	Zinc	Chromium
Sulfur		Selenium	Manganese
		Copper	Molybdenum

Prevent Dehydration	
Events when more water is needed	Extended physical activity Intensive physical activity Humid or hot conditions
What to do	**Prehydrate**—drink two or three cups of cold water two hours before and two cups of cold water ten minutes before event **Hydrate**—drink during the event to quench thirst and renew hydration **Rehydrate**—drink two cups of cold water after the event

Serving Portions
CHAPTER 4 • Physical Growth

Meats (2–3 servings)
1 Serving =

2–3 oz. cooked meat, poultry, or fish

2–3 eggs

1–1½ c. cooked legumes

4–6 tbsp. peanut butter

⅔–1 c. nuts

Hint: Remove visible fat. A 2–3 oz. portion is similar in size to the palm of the hand.

Milk (3 servings)
1 Serving =

1 c. milk, yogurt, milk shake, ice milk, custard, ice cream

1½ oz. cheese

2 oz. processed cheese

Hint: Seek low-fat sources. Try to drink a glass of skim milk with each meal.

Fruits (2–4 servings)
1 Serving =

1 medium apple, orange, banana, peach, pear

½ grapefruit, melon wedge

¾ c. fruit juice

½ c. berries

½ c. canned fruit

¼ c. dried fruit

Hint: Eat whole fruits rather than processed fruits. Eat citrus, berries, kiwi, or melons for Vitamin C daily.

Vegetables (3–5 servings)
1 Serving =

½ c. raw or cooked vegetables

1 c. leafy vegetables

½ c. cooked legumes

¾ c. vegetable juice

Hint: Choose and eat vegetables that are deep green or deep yellow.

Grains (6 or more servings)
1 Serving =

1 slice of bread

½ c. cooked cereal, rice, or pasta

1 oz. ready-to-eat cereal

½ bun or bagel

Hint: Select whole grains and avoid grains with added fats and sugars.

Weight Control
CHAPTER 4 • Physical Growth

Tips for Healthy Eating

- Eat a variety of nutrient-dense foods.
- Use the Food Guide Pyramid to keep track of your consumption and needs.
- Drink water and milk with every meal and with snacks.
- Eat or drink a serving of a food high in vitamin C daily and of a food high in vitamin A every other day.
- Lower your consumption of saturated fat and sugar.
- Use herbs and spices rather than creamy or buttery sauces to season foods.
- Eat slowly. It takes time for your stomach to signal the brain that it is full.

Well-Balanced Fitness Program

Aerobic exercise every other day	5–10 min. warm-up 30 min. aerobic exercise 5–10 min. cool-down
Strength training exercise every other day	5–10 min. warm-up 20–30 min. strength training exercise 5–10 min. cool-down One day for sports (swimming, bicycling, hiking)

On Target
CHAPTER 4 • Physical Growth

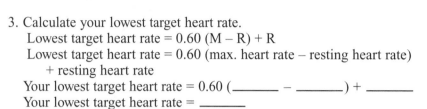

1. Determine your maximum heart rate (220 – your age).
   Your maximum heart rate = M = _____

2. Find your resting heart rate by counting your pulse just before getting up in the morning. (Place your index and middle fingers on either side of the Adam's apple on your neck. Count how many beats per minute by watching the second hand on the clock.)
   Your resting heart rate = R = _____

3. Calculate your lowest target heart rate.
   Lowest target heart rate = 0.60 (M – R) + R
   Lowest target heart rate = 0.60 (max. heart rate – resting heart rate) + resting heart rate
   Your lowest target heart rate = 0.60 (_____ – _____) + _____
   Your lowest target heart rate = _____

4. Calculate your highest target heart rate.
   Highest target heart rate = 0.80 (M – R) + R
   Highest target heart rate = 0.80 (max. heart rate – resting heart rate) + resting heart rate
   Your highest target heart rate = 0.80 (_____ – _____) + _____
   Your highest target heart rate = _____

5. Work up to your highest target heart rate. Check your pulse periodically and keep within your target heart rate zone. If your pulse is beating above your maximum heart rate, slow down, lessen the intensity, or change the activity. If your pulse is below your lowest target heart rate, increase your intensity (go faster, increase the incline, or increase the weight).

6. You should do this three times a week for at least twenty minutes. Chart your progress in order to keep on target.

7. Star all days that you exercised within your target zone.

Day / Date	/	/	/	/	/	/
Time spent in warm-up						
Heart rate after warm-up						
Type of aerobic exercise done						
Heart rate after 10 minutes exercise						
Total time spent in exercise						
Final heart rate after exercise						
Time spent in cool-down						
Heart rate after cool-down						

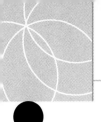

Posture Goals

CHAPTER 4 • Physical Growth

In order to look your best, consider your posture. Do you need to work on your posture in general? Are you one who tends to slump in your chair or church pew? Do you need to practice walking in proper alignment? What are the major areas that you need to work on to improve your posture? For the next five weeks, select five posture-related problems that you want to fix. Work on one goal the first week, then add another goal the second week. Each week you will add another goal, but still be responsible for implementing previous goals.

Step I: Establish your purpose.

The reason I want to achieve my posture goals is that _____

_____.

Step II: Support your purpose with a reference and verse from the Bible (write out the entire verse as it appears in the Bible).

_____

_____

_____

_____

Step III: List areas that need improvement in posture (sitting, standing, or walking).

_____   _____

_____   _____

_____   _____

_____   _____

_____   _____

Step IV: Number the list above in order of difficulty.

If you are constantly slumping, work on this first. Correct more specific problems (sitting with legs extended, swinging arms as you walk, bouncing as you walk, leaning rather than standing, etc.) toward the end of the project.

Step V: Restate each problem in the form of a goal to be accomplished.

List your goals on the chart in order of difficulty.

Step VI: Determine a specific plan for how you can achieve each goal.

Step VII: After each week, take time to evaluate yourself.

Did you achieve your goal? Were you consistent in following the plan? Was it a good plan (Too easy? Too difficult?)? Were there benefits or problems?

Posture Goals, cont.

CHAPTER 4 • Physical Growth

Posture Goals Record

Week	1	2	3	4	5
Goal					
Plan					
Evaluation					

Physical Enhancement

Scents and Nonsense

Perfume (extract, extrait, or essence) 10–25% perfume oil
Cologne (toilet water) 2–6% perfume oil
After-shave lotions (splash colognes) 0.5–2% perfume oil

Myths

- Fragrance will camouflage body odor. *(The fragrance of cleanliness is better than too much perfume or after-shave.)*
- "The more the better" applies to fragrance. *(This is true only when a scent is in the bottle; on a person, just a little dab will do.)*
- Perfumes come from natural sources. *(Essential oils are derived from plants and animals; however, fragrance oils are compounded in a laboratory. Because so much plant material is needed to extract a small amount of oil, essential oils are usually the most expensive.)*
- Evaporation is the only danger to bottled scents. *(Heat and light can also be damaging.)*
- One should apply perfume by spraying it into the air and then walking under the mist. *(The chemicals in perfumes can often cause fabrics and jewelry to deteriorate or be discolored. Breathing in perfumed mist is not healthful either. Perfume should be sparingly applied to the pulse spots of the skin (inner wrists, throat, etc.).)*

Cleaning Tips for Hair Equipment

- Remove all visible hair (use scissors to cut away tangled hair at the base of brushes).
- Apply shampoo to wash combs and brushes.
- Soak equipment in warm, soapy water.
- Use the brushes to scrub the teeth on combs and the bristles and bases of other brushes.
- Rinse thoroughly with hot water.
- Place brushes bristle-side-down on a towel to dry.

Physical Enhancement, cont.

CHAPTER 5 • Physical Enhancement

Shoe Savvy

Before purchasing a pair of shoes, check for the following qualities.

- Breathability of the uppers to allow sweat to dissipate (The more moisture retained by the shoe, the greater risk for bacterial and fungal growth, which causes stench.)
- Flexibility under the ball of the foot (ability of the shoe to reflect the foot's walking motion)
- Shock absorption (ability to cushion the foot at the heel and the forefoot)
- Stability, to keep feet in alignment (ability to correct the foot's tendency to roll inward or outward)
- Support of the arches (ability to cradle the foot and uphold the arches)
- Weight of shoe (the lighter the better as long as support and stability remain)
- Type of tread (influences safety since slick soles or extra-heavy tread tends to slip)
- Comfort (not pinching or pressing the foot)
- Minimal care required (resists water stains; easily cleaned; no scuff marks left)

After purchasing shoes, use the following shoe and footcare hints.

- Occasionally remove all traces of perspiration and dirt by cleaning the insides of the shoe with rubbing alcohol.
- Replace shoes as the cushioning wears out (especially in athletic footwear).
- Inspect your feet for signs of irritation (redness, blisters, etc.).
- Apply a lotion containing either lanolin or petroleum jelly after bathing to keep the skin on your feet supple.
- Change socks and hose daily.

Shopping Tips

- Carry a brief list of items that you need to complete your wardrobe.
- Look for sales, but remember that a sale item is a bargain only if you need that item.
- Avoid impulse buying.
- Patronize better quality stores and wait until they reduce their quality merchandise.
- Always try on a garment before you purchase it. Make sure it fits well; move, sit, and stretch in it to make sure it has plenty of ease for comfort.
- Read garment care labels and consider dry-cleaning expenses.
- Check for good workmanship.
- Plan your shopping trips to save time and energy.

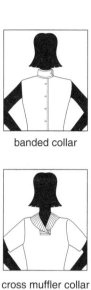    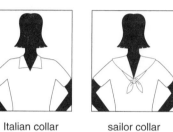

| banded collar | mandarin collar | military collar | pipe collar | ascot collar |

| cross muffler collar | shawl collar | sideways collar | Italian collar | sailor collar |

| peter pan collar | bermuda collar | puritan collar | polo collar | stand-away collar |

 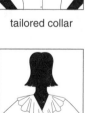 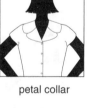  

| convertible collar | tailored collar | petal collar | round collar | shirt collar |

| bow collar | cascading collar | notched collar | button-down collar | ulster collar |

Name

sleeveless

French

cap

petal

set in

pagoda

drop shoulder

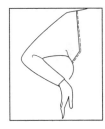

wedge

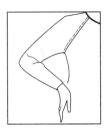

raglan

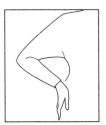

dolman

batwing

puff

balloon

peasant

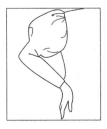

leg of mutton

bateau

crew

square

sweetheart

v

cardigan

jewel

funnel

choker

turtle

Elements of Art

CHAPTER 5 • Physical Enhancement

Test your understanding of the elements of art and the principles of design. Follow the given directions and compare your completed sheet to the teacher's visual, which will be shown in class.

Form: Identify the three basic dress shapes—bell, triangular, and tubular.

_____   _____   _____

Color: Color the circles according to the color scheme.

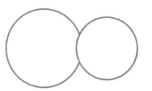 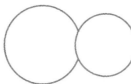 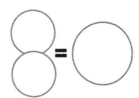 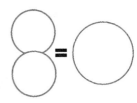

Monochromatic Complementary   Tint   Shade

Line: Color the space between the inner lines the same color.

Texture: Draw or glue a different texture on each square.

Pattern: Draw or glue a different pattern on each square.

Principles of Design

CHAPTER 5 • Physical Enhancement

Proportion: Color the inner parts the same color; leave the outer parts alone.

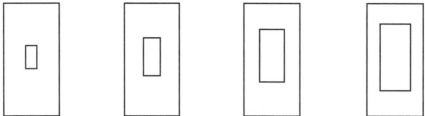

Emphasis: Identify where your eyes are first drawn and circle it on each form.

Rhythm: Identify the type of rhythm that is displayed.

_____ _____ _____ _____

Balance: Draw two pockets on each form according to the given type of balance.

symmetrical   *assymetrical*

Harmony: Describe the clothing outfit you would suggest for your 14-year-old brother to wear when attending a piano recital at your church.

Wardrobe Inventory

CHAPTER 5 • Physical Enhancement

I. Inventory your wardrobe to discover your needs. This can also help you to mix and match your outfits, remove unused clothing, complete needed repairs, and plan for future clothing purchases.

   A. Organize your closet(s), drawers, and storage facilities.
1. Place all items neatly in their proper places.
2. Hang all long items together on one side of the closet.
3. Place all pants/skirts and shirts/sweaters/jackets in groups above the shoes.
4. Arrange caps, ties/scarves, and bags on shelves or organizers.
5. Get a plastic box for cleats, hiking boots, and shoes that may have remnants of mud or grass.
6. Put clothing that needs repairs in a basket.
7. Use a white garbage bag for clothing that can be donated or recycled.
8. Use a dark garbage bag for clothing that cannot be donated or made into rags (must be thrown away).

   B. Categorize your wardrobe. Write the following on divider cards.
1. Clothes
2. Undergarments
3. Home grungy
4. Casual
5. Athletic
6. School
7. Church
8. Formal
9. Shoes
10. Hats/caps
11. Accessories

II. Complete an inventory card for each garment.

Main Category:

Name of item:

Description:

Color:

Condition and Age:

Cost:

   Keep your wardrobe organized and your inventory current.

III. Staple packets of spare buttons to the proper garment cards.

IV. Color the grid on the back of this worksheet to determine your basic clothing needs.

V. Make a list of clothing (and the colors) needed in the future using the information from your color chart.

© 2004 BJU Press. Reproduction prohibited.

Wardrobe Inventory, cont.

CHAPTER 5 • Physical Enhancement

Use crayons, markers, highlighters, or colored pencils to indicate each of the following types of occasions. Then, using these colors as a key, color each hour of the week with the type of clothing usually required for that portion of the day. Compare your needs with your inventory.

Work ☐   Casual Out ☐

Dressy ☐   Casual Home ☐

Sports ☐   Exercise ☐

Time	Sunday	Monday	Tuesday	Wednesday	Thursday	Friday	Saturday
6 A.M.							
7 A.M.							
8 A.M.							
9 A.M.							
10 A.M.							
11 A.M.							
12 P.M.							
1 P.M.							
2 P.M.							
3 P.M.							
4 P.M.							
5 P.M.							
6 P.M.							
7 P.M.							
8 P.M.							
9 P.M.							
10 P.M.							

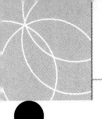

Shopping Tips for Men
CHAPTER 5 • Physical Enhancement

Suits
- Choose solid colors: black, navy, medium gray, medium blue, tan, or camel. Subdued plaids and pinstripes are also good choices. Avoid greens and chocolate brown for dressy occasions.
- Wool/polyester blends are good choices for style and durability. Textured polyester is a good choice if it looks like wool and is neatly tailored.
- Medium-width lapels are the wisest buy.
- Choose straight or slightly flared pant legs.

Shirts
- Blends of 65% cotton and 35% polyester are best; they allow perspiration to evaporate and they resist wrinkles.
- Choose medium-width collars.

Ties
- Choose medium-width ties.
- Silk and polyester that looks like silk are the best fabrics.

Sweaters
- Check the care labels.
- Washable wool and most synthetic sweaters can be home-laundered.
- Regular wool sweaters must be dry-cleaned.
- Loosely knit sweaters stretch easily.

Shoes
- Buy the best quality that you can afford.
- Thin-soled shoes cannot withstand constant wear.
- Choose neutral colors that blend with your wardrobe.
- Black goes with gray, black, and blue.
- Cordovan (red-brown leather) goes with tan, brown, navy, black, and gray.
- Chocolate brown does not match navy, black, or gray.
- The style of shoe should blend with your clothing; do not wear casual shoes for dress.
- Choose styles that flatter your feet.
- Keep shoes shined and in good repair.

Accessories
- Choose small belt buckles.
- Over-the-calf socks are best.
- Wear dark socks that match your slacks or shoes.
- Avoid wool and nylon socks if you get athlete's foot.

Stain Removal Guide
CHAPTER 5 • Physical Enhancement

Fabric reacts to stains in various ways, depending on the types and amounts of fibers that compose the cloth.

Basic Guidelines for Removing Stains

- Attempt to remove stains as soon as possible. The longer they remain, the more difficult it is to get them out. Blot or try to absorb the stain before it sets into the fabric.
- Do not place a stained garment in the dryer or iron over the stain since these actions could heat-set the stain into the fibers.
- Read your clothing care label (or get a copy of the clothing care tag if you purchase fabric to make clothes).
- Always test a stain removal procedure on a scrap piece of fabric or a portion of the garment that cannot be seen.
- Rinse fabrics from the wrong side to flush the stain out of the fabric rather than into the fibers.
- Certain fibers are naturally opposed to some chemicals (acetone [in many fingernail polish removers] disintegrates acetate; perfume, chlorine bleach, and hairsprays can damage silk; chlorine and water can damage rayon; ammonia is bad for wool and silk).
- Always use bleach with detergent in water as hot as possible.
- Do not bleach leather, silk, nylons, spandex, or wool.

Additional Laundry Tips

- Unbutton garments before washing them.
- Turn lint magnets (corduroy, permanent press, or synthetic clothes) and clothing with heat-set lettering inside out before washing.
- Empty all pockets before laundering clothes or sending them to the dry cleaners.
- Do not overload the washer and dryer.
- Decorated items (fur, metallic, sequins, suede, velvet, and vinyl) may be impossible to remove stains from.
- Lingerie and clothing with elastic should be dried on a no-heat setting.
- Do not over-dry garments. They will be less wrinkled if removed from the dryer when barely dry.
- Do not dry white nylon in the direct sun; it may yellow.
- Do not iron velvet; let it hang in a steamy environment on a padded hanger.

If you have any questions or cannot get a stain out, take the garment to a professional cleaner.

Ways to Remove Stains from Washable Fabrics

(If you take your garment to a professional cleaner, explain the nature of the stain [how it got there, when it got there, and what it is]. Specialty fabrics such as velvet, satin, and moiré should be taken to a professional for stain removal.)

Adhesive Tape

Harden the adhesive with ice cubes and scrape the residue with a dull butter knife or spoon. If any remains, saturate the area with stain remover or sponge the back of the area lightly with dry-cleaning fluid with the front portion placed on absorbent paper towels; then rinse and launder.

Barbecue Sauce

Soak stained fabric in cool water as soon as possible; make a paste of detergent and white vinegar on the back side of the stain, then flush with water. Do not heat-set the stain (in a dryer or with an iron).

Blood

Treat with detergent (or a presoak product) and soak in cool water; launder. If the stain persists, use an enzyme cleaner or treat with a few drops of ammonia.*

*Do not use ammonia on wool or silk.

Stain Removal Guide, cont.

CHAPTER 5 • Physical Enhancement

Chocolate

Scrape off any visible residue (not pushing it into the fibers). Apply dry-cleaning fluid and let air-dry. Apply liquid detergent and rinse. Use 3% hydrogen peroxide and a drop of ammonia and launder.

Coffee

Soak in or sponge with cool water as soon as possible; make a paste of detergent and white vinegar for the stain, flush with water, and air-dry.

Dingy White Socks

Presoak in presoak product or laundry detergent and water overnight; launder with detergent and bleach.

Dye

Neutralize the stain as quickly as possible with diluted ammonia* (1 tablespoon ammonia to 1 cup water). Do not place clothing into the dryer until the dye is removed. You may also try soaking the clothing in a water, laundry detergent, and ammonia solution for an hour. Rinse, add laundry prewash, and launder with bleach safe for the fabric.

   * *Do not use ammonia on wool or silk.*

Egg

Treat with detergent (or enzyme presoak product) and soak in cool water; launder.

Fruit Juice

Do not use soap (bar soap, hand soap) or any heat until the stain is gone, since these substances can set the fruit stain. Make a paste of detergent and white vinegar on the stain, flush with water, and air-dry.

Grass

Sponge the stain with alcohol** and then treat with prewash and soak. Rinse and launder with bleach.

   ** *Do not use colored or fragrant rubbing alcohol. Alcohol may cause some dyes to run. Test the fabric first.*

Gravy

Scrape off any visible residue (being careful not to push it into the fibers). Apply dry-cleaning fluid and let air-dry. Apply liquid detergent and rinse. Use prewash and launder.

Grease

Use an absorbent material (cornmeal may be more easily removed than cornstarch or talcum powder) to blot as much of the grease as possible; you may let it remain on fabric all day before brushing it off. Remove any remaining stain by pretreating with a prewash stain remover and launder in warm water.

Stain Removal Guide, cont.

CHAPTER 5 • Physical Enhancement

Gum

Harden the gum with ice cubes and scrape the residue with the dull edge of a knife. If any remains, sponge lightly with cleaning fluid, rinse, and launder.

Ice Cream

Scrape off any visible residue (being careful not to push it into the fibers). Apply dry-cleaning fluid and let air-dry. Apply liquid detergent and rinse. Use prewash and launder.

Ink

Pretreat with a prewash stain remover and launder. (Some inks are impossible to remove.) Sometimes saturating with hairspray and blotting the excess with a clean cloth works on ballpoint ink. Flushing with cool water and sponging ammonia and rinsing often removes India ink. Pretreat, ammonia, and even insect repellent may be needed to remove marker ink (but repellent may damage Spandex, acetate, and rayon).

Ketchup

Soak stained fabric in cool water as soon as possible; make a paste of detergent and white vinegar on the stain, then flush with water. Do not heat-set the stain (in a dryer or with an iron).

Meat Juices

Treat with detergent (or presoak product) and soak in cool water; launder.

Mildew

If possible, wash the garment with chlorine bleach. Check for colorfastness first. If it cannot be treated with bleach, pretreat and launder in the hottest water possible and dry in the sun.

Milk

Apply dry-cleaning fluid and let air-dry. Apply liquid detergent or prewash and rinse. Use prewash and launder.

Mud

Allow the mud to dry, brush off as much dirt as possible, and then pretreat with a prewash stain remover and launder.

Mustard

Soak in cool water as soon as possible; make a paste of detergent and white vinegar on the stain, flush with water, and air-dry.

Pencil Lead

Using a kneadable art eraser, blot the mark, being sure not to stretch or damage the fabric. Pretreat and launder in warm water.

Perfume

Perfume and colognes can burn holes in wool or become permanent markings. Blot as much as possible with cool water. Use laundry pretreat and wash in warm water. If this fails to remove the stain, do not iron or place in the dryer. Sponge with diluted alcohol and launder again.

Stain Removal Guide, cont.

CHAPTER 5 • Physical Enhancement

Perspiration

Treat with detergent (or presoak product) and soak in cool water; launder. Soaking in warm salt water may reduce the amount of stain or odor. Placing white vinegar on the area often reduces old stains. You may also use alcohol or bleach.

Soft Drinks

Soak the garment in cool water. Make a paste of detergent and white vinegar on the stain; flush with water.

Spaghetti Sauce

Soak stained fabric in cool water as soon as possible; make a paste of detergent and white vinegar on the stain; flush with water. Do not heat-set the stain (in a dryer or with an iron).

Steak Sauce

Soak stained fabric in cool water as soon as possible; make a paste of detergent and white vinegar on the stain; flush with water. Do not heat-set the stain (in a dryer or with an iron).

Tape

Scrape off as much as possible; apply a dry-cleaning solvent; peel off stain; launder.

Tea

Tannin-based stains should be soaked in or sponged with cool water as soon as possible. Make a paste of detergent and white vinegar on the stain, flush with water, and air-dry.

Urine

Treat with detergent (or presoak product) and soak in cool water; launder. May need to sponge with soap and water, a salt solution, or diluted ammonia or hydrogen peroxide.

Vegetables

Soak the garment in cool water as soon as possible; make a paste of detergent and white vinegar on the stain, flush with water, and air-dry.

Higher Order Thinking Skills

CHAPTER 6 • Intellectual Growth

Levels of Thinking	Purpose (Skills Involved)
Knowledge	Remembering previously learned material (recall, define, recognize, remember, list)
Comprehension	Interpreting the material (translate, compare, rephrase, describe)
Application	Using the learned material and its principles (solve, construct, classify, demonstrate)
Analysis	Breaking the material down into its component parts for better understanding (determine evidence, draw conclusions, identify causes, outline, diagram, explain)
Synthesis	Putting parts together into a new arrangement (improve, design, organize, rearrange, predict, devise)
Evaluation	Judging the value of the material (appraise, assess, argue, discriminate, contrast, detect)

Five Steps of Decision Making
Identify the problem.
List all the choices.
Identify biblical principles, pray for wisdom, and obtain additional information and godly counsel.
Make your decision.
Act on your decision, take responsibility for it, and evaluate it.

Things I Love to Do

CHAPTER 6 • Intellectual Growth

List fifteen things that you like to do.

Identify with a $ in the second column things that involve earning or spending money.
Note whether the source was your mother (M), father (F), or both (MF).
In the next column signify whether you do this alone (A) or with other people (P).
In the last column indicate if this is a new (N) value that has come within the last five years.

Fifteen Things I Love to Do	$	M/F	A/P	N
1.				
2.				
3.				
4.				
5.				
6.				
7.				
8.				
9.				
10.				
11.				
12.				
13.				
14.				
15.				

Finish the following sentences.

1. On Saturdays, I like to

2. I feel best when people

3. If I had a million dollars, I would

**Go back to the three sentences above and analyze the values exhibited.
Write your values in parentheses.**

Analyzing Standards

CHAPTER 6 • Intellectual Growth

Values result in personal standards.

Look up the following references to identify the standards of each of the following individuals in the Bible.

Values	Reference	Standard
Abraham valued a godly daughter-in-law.	Genesis 24:3–4	Isaac was not to marry a daughter of
Abraham's servant valued his master.	Genesis 24:12	He sought God's leading on behalf of his master
Rebekah valued compassion and hard work.	Genesis 24:18–20	She gave water to a stranger and all his
Ahasuerus valued his power and wealth.	Esther 1:3–7	
Mordecai valued Esther.	Esther 2:7, 11	He loved her as his own daughter and
Haman valued the homage of others.	Esther 3:1–5	He demanded that all bow down to him
Esther valued her people more than her life.	Esther 4:16–5:2	She risked her life to come before the

Biblical Standards

CHAPTER 6 • Intellectual Growth

The Bible provides many standards to help you become a quality servant for God.

Look up the following passages and match the word and verse with the reference.

Proverbs 13:4	I Corinthians 15:58	Hebrews 10:25
Romans 12:11	Galatians 6:9	I Peter 4:9
I Corinthians 4:2	Colossians 3:23	I John 3:17
I Corinthians 14:40	I Timothy 2:9–10	

1. _____ **Organization** ("Let all things be done decently and in order.")

2. _____ **Faithfulness** ("Moreover it is required in stewards, that a man be found faithful.")

3. _____ **Resolve** ("Therefore, my beloved brethren, be ye stedfast, unmoveable, always abounding in the work of the Lord, forasmuch as ye know that your labour is not in vain in the Lord.")

4. _____ **Perseverance** ("And let us not be weary in well doing: for in due season we shall reap, if we faint not.")

5. _____ **Hard work** ("Not slothful in business; fervent in spirit; serving the Lord.")

6. _____ **Diligence** ("The soul of the sluggard desireth, and hath nothing: but the soul of the diligent shall be made fat.")

7. _____ **Enthusiasm** ("And whatsoever ye do, do it heartily, as to the Lord, and not unto men.")

8. _____ **Hospitality** ("Use hospitality one to another without grudging.")

9. _____ **Compassion** ("But whoso hath this world's good, and seeth his brother have need, and shutteth up his bowels of compassion from him, how dwelleth the love of God in him?")

10. _____ **Modesty** ("In like manner also, that women adorn themselves in modest apparel, with shamefacedness and sobriety; not with broided hair, or gold, or pearls, or costly array. But [which becometh women professing godliness] with good works.")

11. _____ **Church attendance** ("Not forsaking the assembling of ourselves together, as the manner of some is; but exhorting one another: and so much the more, as ye see the day approaching.")

Great Goals

CHAPTER 6 • Intellectual Growth

Decide on one goal that you can accomplish within one week in each of the following areas:

- Personal (correspondence, diet, exercise, sleep)
- Spiritual (devotions, verse memorization, witnessing)
- Academic (work on a paper or project, extra reading on subjects)
- Service (something you will do for someone else)
- Family (something extra you will do with or for your family)

List each goal and compose a detailed plan for accomplishing each goal on the chart. At the end of the week, evaluate your progress.

Goal	Plan	Evaluation
Personal		
Spiritual		
Academic		
Service		
Family		

Time Schedules

CHAPTER 6 • Intellectual Growth

In order to compare the various types of time schedules, you will actually plan and use all four different time schedules discussed in your textbook. You have one week in which to complete this assignment. Scan your general schedule or calendar to determine which schedule you think would be most helpful for which day.

Outlook for the Week

Day 1—General Listing (I plan to do this on _____ day.)
Day 2—Block Plan (I plan to do this on _____ day.)
Day 3—Hour by Hour (I plan to do this on _____ day.)
Day 4—Minute by Minute (The busiest one-hour segment of my most demanding day is on _____ day.)

Directions for Each Day

The night before, plan your day using the selected time schedule. (See the examples in your book.)

During the day, refer to your time schedule and do your best to follow it. At the end of each day, evaluate your schedule at the bottom of the paper.

1. Were you able to follow your schedule easily? Why or why not?

2. If you could do this schedule again, would you have changed anything? Why or why not?

3. What could have been improved? How could you have accomplished more?

4. List the time principles you incorporated into the day. (Refer to pp. 98–99.)

Evaluations of the Schedules

After you have completed all the time schedules, write an overall evaluation. Answer the following questions.

1. Which type of schedule did you like best? Why?

2. Which type of schedule did you like least? Why?

3. Did writing these schedules help you to accomplish more this week than usual? Why or why not?

4. What did you learn about yourself and your time usage while writing and using these schedules?

5. Will you plan to incorporate one or more of these time schedules into your daily life? Explain when and why or why not.

Submitting the Project

Make a cover sheet with an innovative title, your name, the class name, and the date.

Place your time schedules and evaluations behind the cover sheet.
Staple or place in a folder according to your teacher's instructions.
The completed project is due _____.

Godly Fellowship

CHAPTER 7 • Social Growth

Find the following references in your Bible and fill in the blanks.
Search for qualities that encourage fellowship with God.

1. John 17:3 "And this is life eternal, that they might _____ the only true God, and Jesus Christ, whom thou has sent."

2. Amos 3:3 "Can two walk together, except they _____?"

3. Habakkuk 3:18 "Yet I will rejoice in the Lord, _____ in the God of my salvation."

4. I John 2:6 "He that saith he abideth in him ought . . . so to _____
_____."

Search for qualities that encourage fellowship with other Christians.

5. I Thessalonians 5:17 "_____ without ceasing."

6. I Thessalonians 5:18 "In every thing _____: for this is the will of God in Christ Jesus concerning you."

7. Hebrews 10:25 "Not forsaking the _____ of ourselves together, as the manner of some is; but _____ one another: and so much the more, as ye see the day approaching."

8. Acts 2:46–47 "And they, continuing daily _____
_____, and breaking bread from house to house, did _____
_____, and having favour with all the people. And the Lord added to the church daily such as should be saved."

9. Malachi 3:16 "Then they that feared the Lord _____
_____: and the Lord hearkened, and heard it, and a book of remembrance was written before him for them that feared the Lord, and that thought upon his name."

10. II Corinthians 8:4 "Praying us with much intreaty that we would receive the gift, and take upon us the fellowship of the _____."

11. Romans 12:13 "Distributing to the necessity of saints; _____
_____."

12. Romans 12:15 "Rejoice _____ that do rejoice, and weep with them that weep."

13. Romans 15:1–2 "We then that are strong ought to bear the infirmities of the weak, and _____. Let every one of us please his neighbour for his good to edification."

14. Galatians 6:2 "_____, and so fulfil the law of Christ."

Traits of a Clique

CHAPTER 7 • Social Growth

- **Interest in inappropriate or insignificant things (unedifying)**

- **Development of mutual admiration (pride)**

- **Entertainment of criticism and hatred (gossip and slander)**

- **Uneasy intensity**

- **Defensiveness (self-righteousness)**

Mouth Warning

CHAPTER 7 • Social Growth

What do the following verses say about the tongue?

Psalm 10:7 "His mouth is full of cursing and deceit and fraud: under his tongue is _____ vanity."

Psalm 12:3 "The Lord shall cut off all flattering lips, and the tongue that _____ _____."

Psalm 34:13 "Keep thy tongue from evil, and thy lips _____."

Psalm 35:28 "And my tongue _____ and of thy praise all the day long."

Psalm 52:2 "Thy tongue deviseth mischiefs; _____, working deceitfully."

Psalm 52:4 "Thou lovest all _____, O thou deceitful tongue."

Psalm 120:2 "Deliver my soul, O Lord, from _____, and from a deceitful tongue."

Psalm 139:4 "For there is not a word in my tongue, but, lo, O Lord, _____ _____."

Proverbs 10:20 "The tongue of the just is _____: the heart of the wicked is little worth."

Proverbs 10:31 "The mouth of the just _____: but the froward tongue shall be cut out."

Proverbs 12:18 "There is that speaketh like _____: but the tongue of the wise is health."

Proverbs 12:19 "The lip of truth shall be _____: but a lying tongue is but for a moment."

Proverbs 15:2 "The tongue of the wise useth _____: but the mouth of fools poureth out foolishness."

Proverbs 21:23 "Whoso keepeth his mouth and his tongue keepeth _____."

Proverbs 25:11 "_____ is like apples of gold in pictures of silver."

Proverbs 26:28 "_____ those that are afflicted by it; and a flattering mouth worketh ruin."

Proverbs 28:23 "He that rebuketh a man afterwards shall find more favour than he that _____."

Proverbs 31:26 "She openeth her mouth with wisdom; and in her tongue is the _____."

Good Communicators

CHAPTER 7 • Social Growth

A good listener

- pays attention.
- displays interest.
- refuses to interrupt.
- stays focused; is not composing a response.
- seeks clarification.
- notes the speaker's tone and attitude.
- does not jump to conclusions.
- employs critical but not cynical thinking.
- restates the major ideas.
- shows appreciation for the speaker.
- reacts appropriately.

A good speaker

- has a sense of humor.
- displays tact and good taste.
- deletes unnecessary details.
- avoids repetition of stories or phrases.
- does not enter self-centered discussions.
- draws others into the conversation.
- is sensitive to the needs of others.
- keeps from being too personal or offensive.
- remains undemanding.
- displays genuine interest in others.
- stimulates others with new ideas and interests.
- does not take himself too seriously.
- employs good grammar.

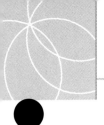

Netiquette
CHAPTER 7 • Social Growth

1. Always place a brief but descriptive header in the subject box.

2. Identify yourself and the URL or website to which you are responding.

3. Be considerate. (Ask yourself how you would feel if you received the message that you are sending.)

4. Be tactful; your words may be used against you. Beware of what you send and save.

5. Avoid writing with sarcasm since it can easily be misread.

6. Keep messages brief.

7. Do not pass on personal messages without getting permission from the originator.

8. Cite all quotations, references, and sources; respect copyrights and license agreements.

9. Save time for your reader by placing quotations on the original message. (Do not put attachments with attachments with attachments; copy and paste or condense information into your message to keep it all succinct.)

10. You may face penalties from your Internet server if you send chain letters or pass them on.

11. Maintain the highest quality of writing (grammar, spelling, and punctuation). Use your spell checker.

12. Never write a message using all capital letters (considered shouting).

13. Use plain text since some software cannot translate various fonts and symbols.

14. Use *asterisks* around a word to give emphasis.

15. Use emoticons to express tone of voice (look sideways to read the symbols).

    :-) means smiling   ;-) expresses a wink

    :- (indicates a frown   :-D shows laughing

    :-O means surprised

16. Use abbreviated comments (acronyms) sparingly.

    FYI—For your information   IMHO—In my humble opinion

    BTW—By the way   LOL—Laughing out loud

    ROFLOL—Rolling on floor laughing out loud

17. Keep your Christian testimony and avoid sending heated messages.

18. Do not send large attachments without getting permission from the recipient first.

Family Communication

CHAPTER 7 • Social Growth

Do the following statements apply to you? Mark each statement *T* for True or *F* for False. Then check your impressions against those of your family. Fold your paper to hide what you wrote and let your family evaluate you.

My Opinion	My Family's Opinion	Checklist
		1. I clearly say what I mean.
		2. I am an attentive and sympathetic listener.
		3. When I do not understand something, I ask a question.
		4. I let other people finish talking before I speak.
		5. I am straightforward and forthright in expressing my thoughts and feelings to others.
		6. I rarely use sarcasm and insults.
		7. I willingly listen to the ideas and feelings of others.
		8. When stating an opinion, I use words like "I think" and "It seems to me."
		9. I seldom get angry or hostile when someone disagrees with me.
		10. I am sensitive to nonverbal signals like tone of voice and body language.

Evaluation

1. Which listening skills need improvement?

2. What are specific ways to improve these?

3. Do any of my speaking skills need improvement?

4. How could I address these specifically?

5. Are there any other aspects affecting my communication that need work (pride, godly self-concept, heart attitude toward God, respect for parents, consideration for siblings)?

    YES   NO

   If so, list these areas in your devotional book. Pray that the Holy Spirit will work in you to cleanse and change your heart. Select portions of Scripture that will help you to remedy these problems. Make apologies if necessary. Have you done all these things?

    YES   NO

Top Tips
CHAPTER 8 • Social Protocol

A tip is a gratuity or show of appreciation for services. Check your bill. Sometimes gratuity has already been added to the bill as a service charge; a tip is not to be added to a service charge. Never be extravagant or stingy. Give an appropriate amount with a tract, a smile, and few or no words. Always calculate the tip on the cost before adding taxes.

Service	Suggested Tip
Airport	
Electric Cart Driver	$1–2 for the driver
Skycap	$1 per bag
Barber Shop/Beauty Salon	
Barber/Stylist	15 percent
Manicurist	$1 or more
Shampooer	$1–2
Deliveries	
Flowers	$2–5
Food (pizza, subs, etc.)	$1–5
Food/Restaurant	
Buffet	5–10 percent
Car Attendant	$1
Coat Check Attendant	$1
Maitre d'	$5–10
Restroom Attendant	$.50–1.00
Servers at Counters	15 percent
Valet Parking	$2 minimum
Waiter/Waitress	15–20 percent
Hotel	
Bellhop	$1 per bag or $5–10
Chambermaid	$1–5
Concierge	$5–10
Room Service	15 percent
Shoeshine	$.50 minimum
Supermarket	
Bagger	$1
Loading the Car	$1–5
Transportation	
Limousine Driver	20 percent
Taxi/Tour Bus Driver	15–20 percent

Rules Mom Taught

CHAPTER 8 • Social Protocol

1. Don't speak with food in your mouth.

2. Don't wave your flatware about when conversing.

3. Remove all food from your fork or spoon as it exits your mouth.

4. Do not place food or used flatware on the table.

5. Make sure that your mouth is empty before getting a drink.

6. Do not touch any part of your body from your shoulders up.

7. Do not blow your nose into your napkin.

8. If you must leave the table, leave your napkin on your seat.

9. Remove bones, pits, and undesirables unobtrusively.

10. Keep your elbows down at your sides.

11. Ask for items to be passed; do not reach past your cover.

12. Do not salt (or season) your food before tasting it.

13. Unless they are provided, do not ask for ketchup, pickles, jam, or sauces.

14. Always try the foods served.

15. If you do not like something, do not let anyone know it.

16. Do not ask for seconds unless they are offered.

17. Signal that you are finished eating by placing utensils across your plate.

18. Remember that the hostess takes the last bite at the meal; do not keep her waiting.

19. Place your used napkin to the left of your plate when you leave the table.

20. Express your gratitude by writing a thank-you note within a week.

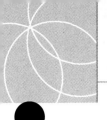

Being a Good Guest

CHAPTER 8 • Social Protocol

Use the following words to complete the sentences below.

6 P.M.
a letter of apology
an appropriate gift
answer the phone
belongings neatly in your suitcase
expected
four days

keep out of family business
leave it as clean
standards or health
take the family out to dinner
to leave first
two hours

For a meal or party

Keep your appointment. Unless you are extremely ill or detained by the law, be sure to arrive at the appointed place at the appointed time. If there is a valid reason for not attending (not feeling like it and because "so-and-so" will not be there are not valid excuses), call to let your hostess know that you will not be attending and why. The telephone call should be followed by _____ within a week.

Be on time. There really is no such thing as "fashionably late." If you are invited to dinner at 6 P.M., you should arrive at _____. You should never arrive earlier or later than the given time.

Be adaptable and agreeable. No one should know whether you do or do not like an activity or a food. As long as your _____ is not compromised, do what is planned and eat what is served. Your host or hostess is trying to be considerate of you; be considerate in return.

Seek thoughtful actions. Look for ways to be thoughtful. Wipe your feet before entering the house; do not interrupt the host and hostess when they are trying to complete a task; do not _____ unless asked to do so; and do not bring or do anything unexpected.

Do not overstay. If you are the guest of honor, you are obligated _____ _____. Unless the dinner was a long and formal dinner, it is normal to remain for about an hour after the meal. However, the entire visit should last about _____ (unless the entertainment was extended in time).

For an extended stay

Do not arrive uninvited. Always make sure that you are _____. It is not considerate to "surprise" your host or hostess.

Bring a hostess gift. Bring _____ for the hostess. Candles, plants, flowers, books, CDs, games, or vases are some ideas for gifts.

Be considerate. Do not keep your host or hostess up late talking, watching television, or playing games. Use the minimum time in the restroom and _____ _____ as when you went in.

Communicate. Find out what plans your host or hostess has for you. Communicate any plans you have and whether you will be missing a meal. If you want to _____ _____, make plans with them ahead of time.

Keep your room clean. Make your bed daily and keep all your _____ _____ or in the space provided for you.

Keep out. Do not pry into the personal belongings of your host or hostess. Because you are a guest in the house, you also need to _____ _____. Give family members their privacy. Knock and wait for an answer before you enter a room.

Do not overstay. Unless you are a close relative, you should not stay longer than _____.

Cover and Buffet

CHAPTER 8 • Social Protocol

Cover

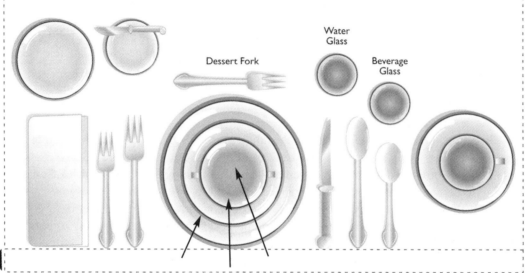

Salad Plate   Bread Plate

Dessert Fork

Water Glass

Beverage Glass

1" from table edge ◄

Napkin   Salad Fork   Place Fork   Dinner Plate   Liner   Soup Bowl   Place Knife   Place Spoon   Soup Spoon   Cup and Saucer

Buffet

Plates   Main Dish / Meat   Starch or Vegetable   Vegetable   Salad   Condiments   Bread   Butter   Napkins & Flatware   Beverage

Planning a Party

CHAPTER 8 • Social Protocol

Kind of Party
Formal
Informal
Snacks
Dinner
Drop-in
Entertainment
Dessert

Theme
Birthday
Holiday
Seasonal
Foreign
Regional
Historical
Emotion
Sports

Guests
Space at party location
Money available
Experience of entertaining
Equipment needed
Whom to invite

Date and Time
Consider your schedule.
  Check school schedule
  Check church schedule

Menu
Variety of foods
Preparation time
Storage facilities

Decorations
Creative but tasteful
Name tags/place cards at the table
Arrangements at table, serving area, entry
Consistent theme presentation
Within budget

Planning a Party, cont.
CHAPTER 8 • Social Protocol

Entertainment
Eating and conversation
Background music
Activities

Invitations
Should include the
- Type of party
- Day of the week and calendar date
- Time (A.M. or P.M.)
- Place (address and location, map or directions included if necessary)
- Host/hostess
- Special Information
- RSVP *(Respondez S'il Vous Plait)*—to whom and by when
  OR
  Regrets Only—Phone Number

Documentation
Take pictures
Make a video
Keep records of plans and evaluation
Make a tape recording of messages or songs by guests

Table Setting Plans
Dinnerware needed for each person
Flatware needed for each person
Glassware needed for each person
Linens needed for each person
Serving bowls/platters/utensils

*Diagram of buffet or dinner table and guest seating assignments
*Diagram of individual cover

Group Plans
CHAPTER 9 • Before Marriage

Goal

You will design a plan for your youth group at church or for friends at school in which everyone can have fun as a group without couples pairing off together. Strive for originality, edification of the saints, and clean Christian fun.

Youth Group Welcoming Party (13-year-olds finished with jr. high)

Event

Theme: _____

Date: _____

Time: _____

Location: _____

(Plan B location in event of rain for outdoor event): _____

Cost for guests: _____

Instructions *(What are guests to wear?)*: _____

Invitations

    Designed by (person): _____

    Distributed by (person): _____

    Date to send (day and date): _____

Include a sample invitation. The invitation should reflect the theme. Be sure to include the event/theme, day/date, time, location, cost, extra instructions, and the host or hostess in charge. It would be an encouragement to parents if a list of adults attending or hosting were included in the invitation.

Activities

As guests arrive: _____

Main thematic activity: _____

Before food is served: _____

Entertainment while guests eat: _____

Following the meal: _____

To end the event: _____

As guests leave: _____

_____

Meal

Appetizer: _____

Entrée: _____

Accompaniments: _____

Dessert: _____

Beverage: _____

Group Plans, cont.
CHAPTER 9 • Before Marriage

Setup
Diagram of
location setup:

Diagram of buffet
or dinner tables:

Diagram of individual
table settings:

Checklist
Enough activities planned? _____

Ample chaperones and help secured? _____

_____

Adequate lighting, ventilation, and shelter considered? _____

Appropriate background music to enhance theme? _____

Sufficient parking places provided? _____

Plenty of help for setup, activities, and cleanup? _____

   (Make a list with phone numbers, addresses, and e-mail addresses. You can use this list to remind helpers of their arrival time, duties, and dress requirements. You can later use the information to write thank-you notes for their assistance.)

Equipment needed to
Decorate
    Entry: _____

    Food area: _____

    Activity area: _____

    Outside area: _____

Set Up
    Tables: _____

    Chairs: _____

    Screens/dividers: _____

    Other items: _____

Group Plans, cont.

CHAPTER 9 • Before Marriage

Serve meal

Serving platters/bowls: _____

Serving utensils: _____

Ice bowls/chests: _____

Pitchers: _____

Condiments: _____

Eat meal

Plates/trays: _____

Salad plates: _____

Bowls: _____

Flatware: _____

Napkins: _____

Dessert plates: _____

Cups: _____

Accomplish the activities:

_____

_____

_____

Clean up after the event:

_____

_____

With Christlike Character

CHAPTER 9 • Before Marriage

Do you desire to have a future mate who exemplifies Christlikeness? You have probably heard others say or have thought to yourself, "I want to marry someone who is like Christ." But what specific characteristics would this entail? What qualities are Christlike? Search I Corinthians 13 to find the character qualities of Christ that you should desire in your own life (as a potential spouse) as well as in the individuals you date.

Read I Corinthians 13 aloud. Every time you see the word *charity*, substitute the word *Christ*. God is love, and Christ is God, therefore, Christ is love (charity).

"He that loveth not knoweth not God; for God is love. In this was manifested the love of God toward us, because that God sent his only begotten Son into the world, that we might live through him." I John 4:8–9

List the qualities that exemplify Christlike character.

Verse 1. _____

_____

Verse 2. _____

_____

Verse 3. _____

_____

Verse 4. _____

_____

Verse 5. _____

_____

Verse 6. _____

_____

Verse 7. _____

_____

Verse 8. _____

_____

Verse 13. _____

_____

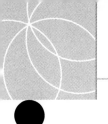

The History of Engagement

CHAPTER 10 • During Engagement

History of Engagement: Father to Father

The two middle-aged men leaned toward each other in the yellow lamplight. Each knew the other's intent; each also knew the value of pushing for a good bargain. "My old friend," began the man with the dark blue jacket, "I understand you have a daughter."

"Ah, yes," the other replied from behind a thick black mustache. He knew that his friend in the dark blue coat had watched the girl grow up and flourish into a lovely young woman, and he knew the other man had a son of marriageable age. "I have a daughter."

"I have a son who is strong, quick-witted, and the pride of his mother and me."

"I have seen your son," the black mustached man replied without betraying too much enthusiasm.

The dark-blue-coated man sat silently in the quietness of the room. He knew that his son needed a hard-working, levelheaded wife like his friend's daughter. He also knew that his old friend loved his daughter very much. He would want the best husband possible for her.

Below the black mustache a slight smile appeared, for the son in question was indeed a good man, and the daughter would need a strong husband, for she was strong-willed. Slowly the man said, "Our families have been friends for many years."

The dark blue coat relaxed visibly as the conversation continued. "My son needs but one thing to make his happiness complete. . . ."

The idea of fathers' arranging the marriages of their children may be hard for you to imagine, but for centuries parents have done so. Even today in many parts of the world two fathers meet to arrange for their children's marriage. They will inform the couple only after they have maturely, lovingly, and thoughtfully considered what will be best for their children.

Abraham had a son whom he loved greatly. He loved his son so much, in fact, that he refused to let him marry one of the pagans who lived near him. Abraham arranged to get his son Isaac a wife. Rebekah "became his wife; and he loved her" (Gen. 24:67).

History of Engagement: Suitor to Father

The rough pavement was wet with the light rain that had blanketed the city for days. Traffic was light, and the tables under the café's canvas awning were quiet except for the respectful voice of the young man.

The older man leaned back in his wooden folding chair as a mighty judge might when considering a condemned criminal. The speaker was not relaxed. "I am a good carpenter," he continued, uncomfortable with his long speech and the unnatural lack of humility it had required. "I am making as much money now as my father was making when he was married." He noticed the older man eyeing the new clothes he was wearing. He hoped they testified to his prosperity. Then, sensing the unasked question, he quickly added, "I have saved money, too. I try to save twenty percent of my weekly pay so that someday I can buy a house and workshop of my own." The young man paused as he tried to think of more reasons that he should be considered a good prospective husband. His speech had sputtered to a close. If he had reflected on the halting delivery and disconnected logic of his presentation so far, he would probably have given up in humiliation, yet he continued.

"Sir, I would like to marry your oldest daughter."

The older man raised his eyebrows now only for the benefit of the young suitor. Actually the surprise had been experienced months before when the young man asked permission to court his daughter.

The father loved his daughter very much and wanted to make sure she would be well provided for and well loved. He planned to accept the youth's proposal, but he wanted to be convinced. "Tell me again. Why do you think you are good enough for *my* daughter?"

As the young man began again, the afternoon sun broke through the last of the rain clouds.

When Jacob asked Laban for Rachel, he had seen her and loved her; but Scripture does not indicate how Rachel felt about Jacob (Gen. 29:1–28). All that is known is that she trusted her father's choice. Even today in many places in the world, well-educated, beautiful girls do not expect to be courted but only to be married to the men their fathers select. They have learned to trust their fathers for the material needs and emotional leadership they have needed while growing up, and they are willing to accept their fathers' choices for life partners.

History of Engagement: Suitor to Maid

The full orange moon softly revealed the details of the well-kept yard as the young suitor sat on the front porch steps. From the house came the sound of her parents' conversation, from the grassy yard came the singing of crickets, and from his side came her sigh. "What a lovely moon!"

"Yeah," he responded. For the next few moments he stared at the moon as if looking for operating instructions.

"How was work today?"

"Just fine," he answered. His voice betrayed the frustration he felt at not knowing how to start the conversation he had planned for so long.

The day before he had met with her father after work and had "The Talk." He had presented his intentions and was pleased that the older man had readily given his permission.

Looking at his feet during the long pause, he finally raised his nerve to speak. He cleared his throat. "I want to talk to you . . . " His heart was beating the way it had on his first date as he clenched his hands tightly to draw courage. Face muscles tense, he looked straight into her sparkling eyes. He saw not the best outfielder on her team, not the elegant lady he had taken to the Senior Banquet, not even the computer analyst who had graduated summa cum laude. He looked into the eyes of the person he had trusted with his dreams, the girl he wanted to protect and cherish, the woman he loved. The tension left his face and throat, and his hands relaxed. He spoke now not in the tense sharps of adolescence, but in the modulated tones of maturity.

"You know that I love you, and I know we've talked some about the future, but I want to make it official. Will you marry me?"

Her eyes glistened in the light of the luminous moon—a moon they would describe to their children and their grandchildren.

Boaz saw Ruth in the field; he began to care for her. She responded to his attention and concern, and their family would bear the kings of Judah and the Lord of glory.

Diamond Mind

CHAPTER 10 • During Engagement

Facets (Plane Facts)

Diamond quality is better than diamond quantity.

The carats (the unit weight) make a diamond more visible, but it is the quality of the diamond that makes it exquisite. In much the same way, a fiancé or fiancée may look good, act nice, and be popular, but it is not his or her number of admirers that counts. Check to make sure the depth of Christian quality is there. Do some "fruit" inspection and see how he or she measures up in the fruit of the Spirit.

There is a difference between a cubic zirconia and a diamond.

Although most people cannot tell just by looking, a jeweler can observe the difference almost immediately. A cubic zirconia has a plastic look and a bluish cast throughout the stone. It also weighs 75 percent more than a diamond of the same size. God's choice for your future mate will also be apparent to wise people who inspect the relationship closely. Wait for God's diamond and do not settle for a fake or for second best.

Settings should be appropriate.

Even if the diamond is beautiful and of the highest quality, it can be lost if the setting is not secure. If a perfect diamond is placed in an insecure setting (too few prongs, unprotected positioning, or too soft a metal), the risk of its being lost or damaged is greater. God's strong and protecting hands must secure a couple's place of service. Any place outside His will is a precarious position.

A diamond is not forever.

A diamond is the hardest substance in the world, but it must be cared for. Hardness keeps a diamond from scratching. However, it can fracture, chip, or break. The relationship between a husband and wife is the same. It too must be cared for so that fractures, chips, and breaks do not occur.

Appraisal (Verification)

Several biblical principles are given in the Facets above. Find Bible verses that support each principle, and write out the entire verse and reference.

Diamond quality is better than diamond quantity.

There is a difference between a cubic zirconia and a diamond.

Settings should be appropriate.

A diamond is not forever.

Bride's Timetable

CHAPTER 10 • During Engagement

Bride's Timetable

At Least 6 Months Before

- Purchase an organizer (planner, notebook, file case, computer program, or Internet).
- Discuss wedding plans and budget details with fiancé and both sets of parents.
- Choose a date, time, location, wedding size, and formality.
- Check with local authorities on obtaining a wedding license.
- Make appointments with your pastor for you and your fiancé to get premarital counseling.
- Obtain a wedding director, caterer, photographer, videographer, and florist.
- Select attendants and decide on a color, style, and theme for your wedding and reception.
- Pick out a bridal gown and headpiece (gowns may take 6–12 weeks to arrive).
- Create a bridal registry after you and your fiancé have made your selections (if he lives in another city, register with a store that can keep track of your gifts in both locations).
- Purchase a gift register and/or guest book. Record and acknowledge gifts as soon as they are received.
- Develop a guest list and have your fiancé start his (with addresses) and place these in a computer database that can be used later to make labels for Christmas cards.
- Select the wedding rings.
- Begin to decide on the music you will use for the ceremony.
- Make church, reception hall, rehearsal dinner facilities, and rental (arches, tables, etc.) reservations.

5 to 4 Months Before

- Pre-shop for attendants' apparel with mother or matron/maid of honor to survey for style, color, and cost.
- Make final decisions on your attendants' attire (i.e., gowns, shoes, gloves, jewelry, etc.).
- Schedule bridesmaids' dress and shoe fittings. Select and order attire for groomsmen.
- Make doctors' appointments.
- Arrange transportation to the ceremony and reception sites if necessary.
- Order your wedding cake (may take drawings and pictures of what you want).
- Have mothers choose their gowns. (The mother of the bride usually selects her color and style first.)
- Reserve a block of rooms for out-of-town guests.

3 to 2 Months Before

- Verify florist, photographer, videographer, and caterer specifications.
- Complete your guest list and get your fiancé's list and addresses.
- Order your invitations and stationery (personalized napkins are optional).
- Schedule bridal portrait.
- Meet with wedding consultant and go over final details of the rehearsal, wedding, and reception.
- Finalize honeymoon travel plans (fiancé will usually take care of this).
- Acquire necessary travel documents, including passports, birth certificates, etc.
- Review musical selections with the musicians.
- Address the invitations in proper form. (You may have your mother and/or director help you.)
- Record gifts received and send thank-you notes.
- Plan rehearsal and rehearsal dinner.
- Purchase gifts for bridal party and fiancé (if gifts are being exchanged).
- Schedule final fittings and appointments at the hair salon for attendants and out-of-town guests.
- Obtain wedding props (i.e. pillow for ring bearer, pen[s] for guest book[s], cake knife and server, etc.).
- Prepare the wedding announcement for the local newspaper.
- Finalize the ceremony with the pastor.
- Write place cards for the reception.

Bride's Timetable, cont.

CHAPTER 10 • During Engagement

Bride's Timetable

1 Month Before

- Mail all invitations to allow time for responses.
- Finalize wedding day transportation and confirm accommodations for guests.
- Arrange to change name on driver's license, Social Security card, beneficiary on insurance, etc.
- Ask friend(s) to be guest book attendant(s) and/or receivers for the wedding gifts.
- Select and talk to friends serving as reception hostesses (dress, times, procedures).
- Follow up on guests who have not returned their response cards (get an accurate count for the caterer).
- Meet with your wedding consultant to go over final details of the ceremony procedure.
- Design and check the spelling of your wedding program. Have programs printed.
- Start packing for honeymoon (and your change of address).
- Double-check all details with those providing professional services (photo, video, and flowers).
- Plan seating arrangements for within the ribbons and for rehearsal dinner with director.
- Style your hair with headpiece and practice applying cosmetics in proper light.
- Arrange for one last fitting of all wedding attire. Make sure men's tuxedos fit properly.
- Make sure rings are picked up and fit properly.

3 Weeks to 1 Week Before

- Get marriage license.
- Make arrangements for all the dressing rooms to have ample mirrors, outlets, privacy, space, and décor.
- Know all the details of rehearsal, wedding, and reception.
- Open joint checking and savings accounts; get travelers' checks for honeymoon if needed.
- Mail wedding announcement forms with black and white photos to newspapers.
- Make a final check on your clothing and accessories for wedding and honeymoon.
- If needed, arrange for a police officer to handle traffic.
- Finish writing all thank-you notes possible.
- Inform caterer of final number of guests.
- See your hairstylist for a final trim.
- Have tea or luncheon with bridesmaids.
- Make sure the program is correctly printed and folded.
- Post an arrival schedule of the wedding party (phone numbers of hotel[s]) by the telephone.
- Spend as much time with parents and family as possible.

1 Day Before

- Pamper yourself and have a manicure, pedicure, and facial.
- Lay out everything you need to dress for the wedding in one place at home.
- Have money or checks in envelopes for anyone who needs to be paid at the wedding.
- Attend the rehearsal and rehearsal dinner.
- Do not plan any late-night chats or parties tonight! Get a good night's rest.

Your Wedding Day

- Have a leisurely breakfast and a nice long bath. Take it easy.
- Spend time with out-of-town relatives and your family.
- Graciously thank everyone who helped you.
- Relax, smile, and enjoy! You planned this day carefully and gave the Lord the credit for all He has done. Be calm knowing that He is still in control. Glorify Him in your actions and reactions.

Wedding Plan Summary

CHAPTER 10 • During Engagement

The following wedding plan summary does not contain the answers or setup for every wedding since each wedding is different and individualized for the bride and groom. The plan is a simple tool to help organize the many decisions to be made when planning a wedding. To the best of your ability, answer these questions that should be considered when constructing these plans.

1. If a bride is planning an outdoor wedding or reception, what are some of her options in case of rain? List two ideas.

2. If the bride and groom choose to have two pastors officiating, how should they decide who does what?

3. How does a couple planning a sit-down reception ascertain the number of guests who will be attending so they do not have to pay for the meals of absent guests?

4. Why is it necessary to know the arrival time of the various contractors involved in the wedding?

5. In what way is a junior attendant different from a bridesmaid or groomsman?

6. In what way is an usher different from a groomsman?

Wedding Plan Summary, cont.

CHAPTER 10 • During Engagement

7. What are the advantages and disadvantages of having a flower girl and a ring bearer? Indicate ways that the problems could be alleviated or at least reduced.

8. What would a gift table attendant be required to do? Who would inform the attendant of his or her duties?

9. Why would it be nice to have place cards and seat assignments at the rehearsal dinner?

10. Identify music, a poem, a reading, or a speech that would provide entertainment at a rehearsal dinner.

11. In case one of the rehearsal dinner guests is an alcoholic, where could you have your dinner so that a bar is not available?

12. Plan a menu for a lunch buffet reception for two hundred guests. When selecting foods, consider:
    • cost,
    • ease of preparation and service at a buffet,
    • ability to remain hot or cold, and
    • variety of color, textures, temperatures, flavors, shapes, and food groups.

Wedding Plan Summary, cont.

CHAPTER 10 • During Engagement

Meat or main entrée   Fruit or crisp vegetables

Meat or main entrée   Bread(s)

Starch or accompaniment   Sweet item(s)

Green vegetable   Salty and crunchy item(s)

Red/yellow vegetable   Beverage(s)

13. How many servers are needed at each cake table and what are their jobs?

14. Sketch the location of the serving tables for the best traffic pattern of the guests entering your church reception hall (or your church's courtyard). Consider the proximity of the kitchen for replenishing food, beverages, cups, and dishes.

15. Identify foods that could be served at the pre-wedding buffet for the wedding party. (This is to be a small buffet that is easily set up to provide lunch or breakfast for the wedding party.) Foods should not be messy or have the potential of staining the wedding attire.

16. Who would be in charge of preparing a "food-sample basket" for the bride and groom to take with them on their honeymoon, and why is this a thoughtful item to be incorporated into the plans?

Wedding Plan Summary, cont.

CHAPTER 10 • During Engagement

Day: _____ Date: _____

Place: _____ Estimated number of guests: _____

Rain options for outdoor wedding/reception: _____

Minister(s): _____

Contacts

Contact Information	Home Phone	Work/Cell Phone	E-mail
Bride			
Groom			
Maid or matron of honor			
Best man			

Contractor for:	Name	Phone	E-mail	Arrival Time
Photographs				
Videos				
Audio				
Flowers and greenery				
Reception				
Wedding cake				
Rehearsal dinner				
Bridal gown				
Organ, piano, and other music				
Solo or duet				
Solo or duet				
Instrumental				
Reception music				
Nursery				

Attendants   ## Attire   ## Flowers

Maid or matron of honor
Bridal attendants
Junior attendants
Flower girl
Best man
Groomsmen
Ushers

Wedding Plan Summary, cont.

CHAPTER 10 • During Engagement

Junior attendants
Ring bearer
Guest book attendant
    Guest book location [ ]table/desk [ ]stand [ ]other Time book is to be removed: ____
    Guest book taken to the reception by _____
Program [ ]purchased bulletin [ ]single fold [ ]bi-fold [ ]specialty paper/presentation
    To be taken to the printers by (person and date) _____
    Distribution [ ]by guest book [ ]by ushers [ ]by junior attendants
Gift table attendants
    Table location [ ]foyer [ ]side vestibule [ ]reception hall [ ]gazebo

Flowers

Colors
Theme or style
Type of flowers [ ]silk [ ]real [ ]combination:
Bridal bouquet style
Bridal attendants to carry
Attendants to wear in hair
Flower girl to carry
Floral gift to mothers
Corsages needed [ ]mothers [ ]grandmothers [ ]special [ ]servers [ ]musicians [ ]director
Boutonnieres needed [ ]fathers [ ]grandfathers [ ]attendants [ ]special [ ]pastors
Foyer arrangements
Sanctuary arrangements
Exterior arrangements
Reception arrangements
Cake arrangements

Rehearsal Dinner

Location
Caterer
    Expected number of guests
    Date to notify caterer
Menu

Setup date and time
Setup help
Decorations
Place card calligrapher
Chart of seating arrangement and assignments

Music
Announcer/prayer
Program of events
Cleanup

Wedding Plan Summary, cont.
CHAPTER 10 • During Engagement

Reception Arrangements
Location
Caterer
    Expected number of guests
    Date to notify caterer
Menu

Setup date and time
Setup help
Decorations
Music
Servers

Security during ceremony
Estimated time of arrival following the wedding
Person to take gifts and guest book from church to reception
Cleanup job assignments

Job	Name	Where to Take Item(s)
Check dressing rooms		
Take guest book		
Take bridal gown		
Take tuxedos		
Take cake top		
Take leftover food		
Clean dishes and kitchen		

Church Setup
Changing rooms
    Bride and attendants
    Groom and men
Photography room
Pre-wedding buffet location _____ Served by _____
Exterior
    Doors
    Walkway or landing
Foyer
    Entry décor
    Guest book desk/stand

Wedding Plan Summary, cont.

CHAPTER 10 • During Engagement

Sanctuary
   Chancel
   Stairway
   Windows
   Within-the-ribbons markers
   Pew decorations

Music

Organist
Pianist
Instrumentals
Soloist/Duet/Trios/Choirs
Prelude

Hymn(s)
Grandparents' entry
Parents' entry
Solo music
Processional
Bridal entry
Solo music
Solo music
Recessional

Kneeling bench: when in the service?   Music?
Unity candles: sides lit by [ ]parents [ ]ushers   When?   Music?
Flowers to the mothers [ ]before [ ]after   Type to be given?   Music?

Time and Placement Schedule

Time and place to be ready for photos ____Bride & groom ____Attendants ____Parents
____Pastors ____Family members ____Servers ____Guest book/Gift Table attendants
List and placement of guests within the ribbons

Children allowed?
Mother of the bride [ ]seated [ ]escort bride and dad [ ]stand with bride in front
Placement of bridal party

Receiving line
   Who [ ]parents, bride, & groom [ ]honor attendant [ ]bridesmaids [ ]announcer
   Location [ ]church foyer [ ]church exterior [ ]reception hall [ ]none—mingle [ ]other
Departure
   Bouquet to throw [ ]bridal [ ]extra
   Garter
   Rice/Birdseed [ ]packets [ ]bowls [ ]petals [ ]bubbles [ ]sparklers [ ]other
   Corsage for bride
   Reception basket of guest gifts
Destination or person who knows the destination
Mode of departure: [ ]car [ ]limousine [ ]carriage [ ]antique car [ ]other

Wedding Plan Summary, cont.

CHAPTER 10 • During Engagement

Special Instructions for the Best Man

- Keep the groom calm.
- Assist the groom in getting dressed and arriving on time with the ring and the marriage license. Take responsibility for the bride's ring.
- Make sure that the groom has his boutonniere and is ready for pictures.
- The groom will give you sealed envelopes to pay the preacher, florist, musicians, audio technician, etc. Be sure to deliver these before they leave (some will not be present for the reception).
- Keep the dressing room neat and make sure that the groom's things are in the getaway car.
- Witness the signing of the marriage certificate.
- During the ceremony, watch over the ring bearer.
- Drive the couple to the reception and, if necessary, to the airport after the reception.
- After the ceremony, provide materials needed to "decorate" the getaway car. Be sure that none of the items used will permanently damage the paint or mechanics of the car.
- Place the bride's items in the getaway car (see the maid of honor for this).
- Make sure that the men's dressing room is cleared and that all rental tuxedos are returned.

Special Instructions for the Maid or Matron of Honor

- Keep the bride calm.
- Make sure that the bride has her flowers and is ready for pictures and the ceremony. Be completely dressed in plenty of time to give the bride all your help and attention.
- Take responsibility for the groom's ring.
- Help to watch over the ring bearer and flower girl in waiting room. During the ceremony, watch over the flower girl.
- During the ceremony, hold the bride's flowers. Whenever she turns, quickly and unobtrusively straighten her train for her. Return her flowers to her after the bride and groom kiss.
- Keep the dressing room neat and make sure that the bride's things are placed in the getaway car (see the best man for this). Ensure that the dressing room is cleaned up afterward.
- Make sure that the "food-sample basket" from the reception is in the getaway car.

Directions for the Ushers

- Set the correct mood for the wedding. Be dignified and serious, yet friendly and cordial. Greet each guest that you seat.
- Offer your right arm to
    - the eldest lady in a group of ladies.
    - the mother or wife in a family group; the husband and children should follow.
    - any single lady, whether she is alone or accompanied by a man (the man will follow).
- Hold your arm waist-high and firm.

Wedding Plan Summary, cont.

CHAPTER 10 • During Engagement

- Walk at a normal pace.

- If a man is to be seated, do not offer your arm, but simply walk beside him to seat him.

- Keep the sanctuary as balanced as possible. Friends of the bride are seated on the left and friends of the groom are seated on the right (as you face the chancel). If guests do not state a preference, seat them on either side.

- Once the mother of the bride has been seated, escort no other guests into the sanctuary. Late guests may sit in the back.

Special Seating Instructions

The following people should be seated within the ribbons:

Chancel

_____	_____
_____	_____
_____	_____
_____	_____
_____	_____

Following the Ceremony

- After the parents have been escorted out, guests are directed to leave row by row. The two ushers assigned should extend an open hand toward each pew to indicate that row's turn to leave. Keep at the same pace and row as each other.

- Help to direct guests to the reception. You may also help to transport elderly or handicapped guests to the reception or to their cars.

Reception Instructions

- Report to the reception director for instructions and offer your help.

- Assist guests at the reception. Mingle with the guests.

- Encourage guests to participate in reception activities by being a participant yourself.

- After the reception, assist in loading gifts, decorations, and other items that need to be cleared or moved.

Name _____

Wedding Expenses

CHAPTER 10 • During Engagement

1. Find out what the average wedding budget is in the United States. You can do this by using a search engine on the Internet and typing in the words *average wedding budget USA*. Once you have viewed the answer, do not waste time by scrolling through all the other sites and word combinations given. Usually, you do not need to go to a website at all since the search engine will provide the answer.

2. Using information gathered in class activities or by inquiring at local businesses, find out the lowest cost for purchasing or renting (not making or borrowing) the following items. (Your teacher may choose to divide the list between you and your classmates.) The class wedding will have six attendants for the bride and six for the groom, including the honor attendants, and all the parents and grandparents. You will need one minister, one organist, one three-taper candelabra, four ferns, one floral spray of carnations in the church, one smaller carnation arrangement to be placed at the guest registry in the foyer (and later transferred to the reception), one kneeling bench, five long-stemmed carnations with fern and ribbon for each female attendant, and one basket of petals for the flower girl. There will be no bachelor party or bridesmaids' luncheon. The reception should feed 100 guests and include wedding cake, nuts, mints, and punch. The couple want a bridal portrait and wedding pictures and album (the photographer's smallest package) and will give their attendants silver picture frames (5" × 7").

3. Add up all the wedding expenses and determine the total cost of a low-budget wedding in your area.

Expense Explorations

Apparel	Total	Subtotal
Bride's gown	$	
Bride's veil		
Bride's accessories:		
Shoes		
Slip		
Other		
Attendants' gowns, each $_____		
Flower girl's dress		
Groom's tuxedo rental or suit		
Groomsmen's tuxedos or suits, each $_____		$

© 2004 BJU Press. Reproduction prohibited.

Wedding Expenses, cont.

CHAPTER 10 • During Engagement

Flowers	Total	Subtotal
Bride's bouquet	$	
Attendants' flowers, each $_____		
Groom's boutonniere		
Groomsmen's boutonnieres, each $_____		
Flower girl's flowers		
Ring bearer's boutonniere		
Mothers' corsages, each $_____		
Grandmothers' corsages, each $_____		
Fathers' boutonnieres, each $_____		
Minister's boutonniere		
Musicians' boutonnieres, each $_____		
Corsages $_____		
Reception servers' corsages, each $_____		
Director's corsage		$

Decorations	Total	Subtotal
Church decorations: Greenery	$	
Floral arrangements, each $_____		
Other		
Reception decorations: Greenery		
Floral arrangements, each $_____		
Other		
Rental of arch, kneeling bench, candelabra, etc.		
Other items		$

Fees	Total	Subtotal
Director	$	
Minister(s), each $_____		
Musicians		
Organist		
Pianist		
Instrumentalists (harp, flute, strings, etc.)		
Vocalist(s), each $_____		$

Wedding Expenses, cont.

CHAPTER 10 • During Engagement

Photographs	Total	Subtotal
Bridal portrait	$	
Wedding pictures and album		
Video or digital recordings		
Other		$

Reception	Total	Subtotal
Rental of reception hall	$	
Wedding cake		
Other food: Groom's cake		
Sandwiches		
Fruit		
Vegetables		
Cheese and crackers		
Nuts and mints		
Other		
Beverages: Punch		
Coffee		
Other		
Rental or purchase of plates, cups, flatware, serving dishes		
Napkins		
Other		$

Miscellaneous	Total	Subtotal
Rehearsal dinner	$	
Bridesmaids' luncheon and bachelor party, each $_____		
Wedding rings, bride $_____; groom $_____		
Invitations		
Attendants' gifts, each woman $_____; each man $_____		
Grand Total		$

Shower Plans

CHAPTER 10 • During Engagement

Plan a complete bridal shower that carries out a specific theme. You may get ideas from friends or books, but the work turned in must be your own. You will be graded on three things: 1) how thoroughly your theme is carried out, 2) originality, and 3) neatness.

As you plan this project, have a friend in mind for which you may want to someday give this shower. Remember to be practical; manage your time, energy, and money in your planning. Plan something that you can really use. Enjoy yourself!

I. Select a theme.
   A. Choose from the following or obtain permission from the teacher for an original theme: kitchen, pantry, personal, linen, bathroom, china, yard and garden, home décor, tool and garage, or miscellaneous.
   B. Write your theme on a sheet of paper and turn it in to the teacher by _____.
   C. Arrange every part of this project (invitations, centerpiece, decorations, games, prizes, devotional) to carry out the theme.

II. Make an original invitation.
   A. Hand in two identical invitations (one for you to keep and one for the teacher's files).
   B. Design the invitation to fit into a regular-sized envelope (but no envelope is required).
   C. Strive for neatness in design, cut, coloring, and presentation.
   D. Incorporate the following information:
      1. Name of the girl being honored
      2. Type of shower
      3. Day and date of the shower
      4. Time (Dinner? Brunch? Lunch?)
      5. Location
      6. Name of host or hostess
      7. Gift registry
   E. Include other appropriate information.
      1. RSVP (RSVP = *Respondez S'il Vous Plait* = Respond if you please)
      2. RSVP by _____.
      3. RSVP regrets only
      4. RSVP _____—_____.
      5. Special information (surprise shower, park in neighboring church lot, bring a poem, etc.)
   F. Hand in to teacher two weeks before project is due on _____.

III. Plan the menu.
   A. Write it in correct form.
      1. Main dish(es)
      2. Vegetable(s) or Side Dish(es)
      3. Fruit(s) or Salad(s)
      4. Bread(s)
      5. Dessert(s)
      6. Beverage(s)

Name _____

Shower Plans, cont.

CHAPTER 10 • During Engagement

  B. Include all recipes.
  C. Seek variety (colors, tastes, textures, shapes, and temperatures of food).
  D. Determine how to keep hot foods hot and cold foods cold.
  E. Create garnish and presentation ideas.
   1. Prepare a list of necessary items to purchase or make.
   2. Plan to make garnishes ahead since they take so much time.

 IV. Plan the setting.
  A. Identify the colors to be used.
  B. Draw a diagram of the main buffet table.
   1. Place plates at the beginning of each line; flatware, napkins, cups, and beverage should be at the end.
   2. Sketch the place for each food (usually the same order as given on the menu).
   3. Draw all serving pieces needed for the event. (Draw them to the right of each serving dish.)
   4. In the corner of your paper, note the number of flatware, china, glassware, and linens needed.
   5. Draw the placement of each centerpiece.
   6. Flatware, napkins, and cups are placed at the end of the serving table if not on a separate island or on tables prepared for guests.
  C. Describe or draw the centerpiece.
  D. Tell how the entry and room(s) will be decorated.
   1. What items will be needed?
   2. When is this to be done?
   3. Who will do it?

 V. Write the order of events.
  A. List the activities from arrival through departure of guests.
  B. Plan on having the devotional prior to refreshments (so it will not quiet and sober everyone at the beginning or the end of the party).

 VI. Plan two games.
  A. Write out the complete instructions.
  B. Include a sample of any handouts.
  C. Add a paper with any answers for your game.
  D. List the prizes to be given to the guests. (Winning guests may opt to give their prizes to the bride, but they should not be expected to.)

 VII. Outline a devotional.
  A. Include appropriate Scripture references.
  B. Put enough "meat" in the outline to indicate your complete meaning.
  C. Plan for the devotional to take between five and ten minutes to deliver.

 VIII. Compile the project.
  A. Write or type the required information.
  B. Assemble everything neatly into a notebook.
  C. Make the pages secure.
  D. Hand in complete project on _____ .

Biblical Roles

CHAPTER 11 • After the Wedding

Briefly state in *your own words* what each verse teaches today's Christian wife and husband. Use these characteristics to evaluate your traits as a future husband or wife as well as to measure the qualities of future dates.

Characteristics of a Christian Wife

Proverbs 12:4—A virtuous woman is a crown to her husband: but she that maketh ashamed is as rottenness in his bones.

Proverbs 19:14—House and riches are the inheritance of fathers: and a prudent wife is from the Lord.

Proverbs 27:15—A continual dropping in a very rainy day and a contentious woman are alike.

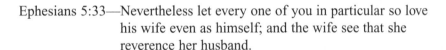

Malachi 2:14b—Yet is she thy companion, and the wife of thy covenant.

Mark 3:25—And if a house be divided against itself, that house cannot stand.

Ephesians 5:33—Nevertheless let every one of you in particular so love his wife even as himself; and the wife see that she reverence her husband.

I Timothy 2:9–10—In like manner also, that women adorn themselves in modest apparel, with shamefacedness and sobriety; not with broided hair, or gold, or pearls, or costly array. But (which becometh women professing godliness) with good works.

I Timothy 3:11—Even so must their wives be grave, not slanderers, sober, faithful in all things.

I Peter 3:1—Likewise, ye wives, be in subjection to your own husbands; that, if any obey not the word, they also may without the word be won by the conversation of the wives.

Biblical Roles, cont.
CHAPTER 11 • After the Wedding

Characteristics of a Christian Husband

Deuteronomy 6:7—And thou shalt teach them diligently unto thy children, and shalt talk of them when thou sittest in thine house, and when thou walkest by the way, and when thou liest down, and when thou risest up.

Romans 12:13—Distributing to the necessity of saints; given to hospitality.

Ephesians 5:23—For the husband is the head of the wife, even as Christ is the head of the church: and he is the saviour of the body.

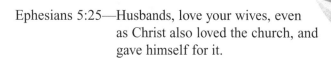

Ephesians 5:25—Husbands, love your wives, even as Christ also loved the church, and gave himself for it.

Ephesians 5:28—So ought men to love their wives as their own bodies. He that loveth his wife loveth himself.

Ephesians 5:31—For this cause shall a man leave his father and mother, and shall be joined unto his wife, and they two shall be one flesh.

Ephesians 6:4—And, ye fathers, provoke not your children to wrath: but bring them up in the nurture and admonition of the Lord.

I Timothy 5:8—But if any provide not for his own, and specially for those of his own house, he hath denied the faith, and is worse than an infidel.

I Peter 3:7—Likewise, ye husbands, dwell with them according to knowledge, giving honour unto the wife, as unto the weaker vessel, and as being heirs together of the grace of life; that your prayers be not hindered.

Applying Proverbs 31 Today

Definition of a Virtuous Woman

"Who can find a virtuous woman? For her price is far above rubies."
~Proverbs 31:10

The term "virtuous woman" can be translated "a woman of strength" or "a woman of power." She is made strong through wisdom, grace, and a fear of God. She has the power to help break or build her husband's life, power to guide the lives entrusted to her in the form of children, power to influence others and be a witness through her life for the Lord.

Though she is strong, she is also weak. She is weaker than her husband ("honor unto the wife, as unto the weaker vessel" I Peter 3:7). She is to submit to him in obedience to God's command ("Wives, submit yourselves unto your own husbands, as unto the Lord" Ephesians 5:22) and as a testimony to the unsaved ("Likewise, ye wives, be in subjection to your own husbands; that, if any obey not the word, they also may without the word be won by the conversation of the wives" I Peter 3:1).

Such a woman of character, talent, and influence is hard to find, and the need is great. She is worth more than gems; she is a valuable asset to her husband, the community, and most importantly, the family of God.

Characteristics of a Virtuous Woman

Read each verse of Proverbs 31:11–31. For each verse listed below, write one or two characteristics of a virtuous woman that a modern homemaker should have. Do not rewrite the characteristics given, but make an application for today's Christian homemaker.

Verse 11 "The heart of her husband doth safely trust in her, so that he shall have no need of spoil."

Verse 12 "She will do him good and not evil all the days of her life."

Verse 13 "She seeketh wool, and flax, and worketh willingly with her hands."

Verse 14 "She is like the merchants' ships; she bringeth her food from afar."

The Christian Homemaker, cont.

CHAPTER 11 • After the Wedding

Verse 15 "She riseth also while it is yet night, and giveth meat to her household, and a portion to her maidens."

Verse 16 "She considereth a field, and buyeth it: with the fruit of her hands she planteth a vineyard."

Verse 17 "She girdeth her loins with strength, and strengtheneth her arms."

Verse 18 "She perceiveth that her merchandise is good: her candle goeth not out by night."

Verse 19 "She layeth her hands to the spindle, and her hands hold the distaff."

Verse 20 "She stretcheth out her hand to the poor; yea, she reacheth forth her hands to the needy."

Verse 21 "She is not afraid of the snow for her household: for all her household are clothed with scarlet."

Verse 22 "She maketh herself coverings of tapestry; her clothing is silk and purple."

Verse 23 "Her husband is known in the gates, when he sitteth among the elders of the land."

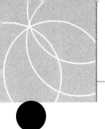

The Christian Homemaker, cont.

CHAPTER 11 • After the Wedding

Verse 24 "She maketh fine linen, and selleth it; and delivereth girdles unto the merchant."

Verse 25 "Strength and honour are her clothing; and she shall rejoice in time to come."

Verse 26 "She openeth her mouth with wisdom; and in her tongue is the law of kindness."

Verse 27 "She looketh well to the ways of her household, and eateth not the bread of idleness."

Verse 28 "Her children arise up, and call her blessed; her husband also, and he praiseth her."

Verse 29 "Many daughters have done virtuously, but thou excellest them all."

Verse 30 "Favour is deceitful, and beauty is vain: but a woman that feareth the LORD, she shall be praised."

Verse 31 "Give her of the fruit of her hands; and let her own works praise her in the gates."

Potential Problems

CHAPTER 11 • After the Wedding

Potential Problem Areas	
Background	
Comes from a poor family	Comes from a rich family
Depends on parents for support	Is independent in nature
Family is openly affectionate	Family is restrained, less demonstrative
Close relationship with family	Has little communication with family
Preferences	
Chills easily	Enjoys the cold
Alert in the morning	Alert in the evening
Enjoys athletic activities	Disdains athletic activities
Values professional appearance	Prefers functional, informal clothes
Emotions	
Does not communicate when angry	Says everything on mind when angry
Enjoys company; is gregarious	Prefers solitude; is shy and retiring
Is meticulous and organized	Is tolerant, flexible, and disorganized
Loses temper easily	Is slow to anger
Has a practical, realistic nature	Has a meditative, reflective nature
Prefers to be early	Uses every moment; may be late
Likes independent work	Likes group work
Finances	
Wants wife in work force	Believes wife should not work outside home
Accepts some debt	Is opposed to debt
Children	
Prefers no children	Wants children
Desires a small family	Dreams of a large family
Wants children right away	Wants to wait for children
Is a strict disciplinarian	Gives children more latitude

Discussing Differences

CHAPTER 11 • After the Wedding

1. Talk to the Lord before talking to your partner about a problem.

2. Keep communication lines open. Pouting and refusing to talk will not solve problems.

3. Maintain a good sense of humor.

4. Never talk about important things when you are tired, angry, or hungry.

5. Do not try to change your spouse. Leave changes to the Lord.

6. Do not overreact or underreact.

7. Keep reactions positive. Expressing anger only feeds it.

8. Do not keep bringing up problems unless you have a solution to offer.

9. If a discussion becomes too intense, table the matter for a while.

10. Be interested in the other person and listen. There is a difference between hearing and listening.

11. Do not let problems pile up.

12. Do not generalize. Be specific about what the problem is and make sure all statements are true.

13. Never use physical or emotional abuse.

14. Never criticize one another publicly.

15. Remember that a question can be the key to the door of communication, but an accusation can lock it shut.

Wise Communication

CHAPTER 11 • After the Wedding

Find the following passages in the Bible and write the verses to see what God has to say about wise communication.

Psalm 141:3

Proverbs 12:25

Proverbs 15:1

Proverbs 15:2

Proverbs 15:23

Proverbs 15:28

Proverbs 17:14

Proverbs 18:23

Proverbs 20:5

Proverbs 20:15

Proverbs 25:9

Proverbs 25:11–12

Proverbs 25:15

Proverbs 29:11

Proverbs 31:26

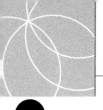

Name _____

Ecclesiastes 12:10

Isaiah 50:4

Romans 13:7–8

Galatians 5:13

Ephesians 4:15, 25

Ephesians 4:26–27

Ephesians 4:29

Ephesians 4:32

Ephesians 5:33

I Peter 3:1–7

Wise Communication, cont.

CHAPTER 11 • After the Wedding

Find the following passages in the Bible and write the verses to see what God has to say about hindrances to wise communication.

Proverbs 11:12

Proverbs 11:13

Proverbs 12:16

Proverbs 12:18

Proverbs 15:1

Proverbs 15:5

Proverbs 16:27

Proverbs 17:9

Proverbs 18:2

Proverbs 18:6

Proverbs 18:8

Proverbs 18:13

Proverbs 18:17

Proverbs 18:23

Proverbs 19:1

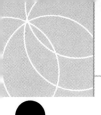

Wise Communication, cont.

CHAPTER 11 • After the Wedding

Proverbs 19:5

Proverbs 20:19

Proverbs 20:25

Proverbs 25:24

Proverbs 26:18–19

Proverbs 26:20–21

Proverbs 26:22

Proverbs 27:2

Proverbs 29:20

Ephesians 4:25

Ephesians 4:29

Ephesians 4:31

Colossians 3:8

Colossians 3:9

Hospitality Ideas

CHAPTER 11 • After the Wedding

When you have the opportunity to witness by opening your home to others, consider doing the following:

1. Greet guests at the door yourself (or with your children). Do not just send the children as if you are too busy or are not ready to welcome them.

2. Never apologize for your house, your menu, your cooking, or your appearance since it may make your guests feel that they have inconvenienced you.

3. Take a moment to sit down with your guests and enjoy them (and let them enjoy you). Get extra help (kitchen help, babysitter, etc.) so that you can enjoy your guests.

4. Offer refreshment to them. This is a good opportunity for children to learn the joy of hospitality by sharing food or at least a drink with guests.

5. Provide fresh cookies. Simply freeze cookie dough in balls that can thaw on a cookie sheet and be baked when needed.

6. Use and give your best to your guest. Do not be stingy or demeaning. This is an opportunity to show Christlikeness.

7. For large groups, have books, photo albums, and games readily available.

8. Do not rush around preparing food. Man's importunities are God's opportunities.

9. Do not hurry through meals. Your times are in His hands.

10. Do not worry about being a good conversationalist. God will give the words to say. Learn how to initiate conversation and to listen.

11. Let children be a part of the adult conversations to provide a chance for them to expand their minds and appreciate your guests.

12. Allow the guests to help if they want to assist you in preparation, service, or cleanup.

13. If unexpected guests arrive, never let it be obvious that they disrupted you.

14. Serve what you have with love. God often uses other people to reveal personal selfishness.

15. Remember that your home is His.

Baby's Layette

CHAPTER 12 • Parenthood

Compare prices and styles for the following items. Choose the best quality for as little money as possible. Determine to be good stewards even though you are not poor. Find the prices for the listed items in your assigned store. Use the nearest discount department store or "supermart" to locate prices for the items not available in your designated store.

Identify the specific location where you located the majority of your items. The research year is _____.

You are to obtain the prices for the baby's layette from

a mall department store	_____
a mall specialty shop	_____
a specialty baby/child shop	_____
a baby supermart	_____
a discount department store	_____
a town department store	_____
consignment shops	_____
thrift stores	_____
newspaper ads and yard sales	_____
Internet sources	_____

	Items to Price		
Number Needed	Class choice of gender _____ Nursery Color _____ Motif _____	**Cost for Each**	**Total Cost**
Room Items			
1	Crib	$	$
1	Mattress		
1	Bumper pad (to keep legs and arms in and to keep drafts out)		
4	Fitted sheets		
2	Mattress pads (waterproof)		
3	Crib pads		
2	Crib blankets, quilts, or comforters (depending on season)		
6	Receiving blankets		
1	Window covering, blinds, and/or curtains (window is 3' × 6')		
1	Glider or rocking chair		
	Page Subtotal		$

Baby's Layette, cont.
CHAPTER 12 • Parenthood

Number Needed	Items to Price, cont.	Cost for Each	Total Cost
	Item		
1	Lamp table (add cost of tablecloth or covering if needed)		
1	Lamp with nightlight		
1	Package of outlet covers		
1	Dresser and/or changing table		
1	Drawer latches		
1	Framed prints or posters		
Bathing			
1	Infant tub or bath support	$	$
8	Infant washcloths		
4	Hooded towels		
1	Package of cotton balls or cotton swabs		
1	Baby no-tears shampoo		
1	Baby soap		
1	Baby lotion or oil		
Diapering			
1	Diaper stacker or basket	$	$
36+	Cloth diapers or		
80+	Disposable infant diapers per week		
1	Box of flushable diaper liners (for cloth diapers)		
1	Diaper pail (to collect soiled diapers)		
1	Trash can		
3	Changing pads		
1	Packet of diaper pins		
1	Tube of baby diaper rash ointment		
1	Cotton ball and diaper pin container set		
1	Box of baby wipes		
	Page Subtotal		$

Baby's Layette, cont.
CHAPTER 12 • Parenthood

Number Needed	Items to Price, cont.	Cost for Each	Total Cost
	Item		
Clothing			
6	Nightgowns and sleepers	$	$
6	Undershirts (snap opening)		
4	One-piece cotton body suits (Onesies)		
4	Waterproof covers for cloth diapers		
1	Sweater		
4	Outfits		
1	Winter bunting or summer sunsuit & 100% UV protection sunglasses		
3	Booties		
3	Pairs of socks		
1	Pair of baby shoes		
2	Hats		
Feeding			
8	4-oz. and 8-oz. baby bottles	$	$
10	Burp cloths or large square cotton cloth diapers		
1	Can powdered infant formula (without iron)		
6	Bibs		
1	Bottle brush		
3	Sets of sippy cups		
3	Sets of plastic baby dishes		
3	Coated baby spoons		
1	High chair		
3	Pacifiers		
2	Pacifier holder tabs		
	Page Subtotal		$

Baby's Layette, cont.

CHAPTER 12 • Parenthood

Number Needed	Items to Price, cont.		
	Item	**Cost for Each**	**Total Cost**
Traveling			
1	Car seat	$	$
1	Cloth neck brace and car seat liner		
1	Infant carrier (front or backpack)		
1	Infant seat		
1	Portable playpen or crib		
1	Stroller		
1	Large diaper bag or backpack		
1	Set of rear window mirrors (to see the baby in the back seat of the car)		
Toys			
1	Mobile or crib toy (check for safety; no strings or cords)	$	$
2	Tub toys		
2	Foot or wrist rattles		
1	Table toy		
3	Learning toys		
3	Infant cardboard or cloth books		
1	Toy box		
1	Playpen		
1	Bouncing seat, stationary exercise center, or play seat		
Miscellaneous			
1	Baby comb and brush set	$	$
1	Blunt pair of baby nail scissors		
1	Nasal aspirator		
1	Rectal thermometer		
1	Petroleum jelly		
1	Bottle baby medicine for fever		
	Page Subtotal		$

Baby's Layette, cont.

CHAPTER 12 • Parenthood

Number Needed	Items to Price, cont.		
	Item	**Cost for Each**	**Total Cost**
1	Medicine dispenser spoon		
1	Bottle of rubbing alcohol (to help the umbilicus dry and fall off)		
1	Teething ring		
1	Gum numbing solution		
1	Swing		
1	Baby gate		
1	Nursery monitor		
1	Smoke and CO detector		
1	Baby food grinder		
1	Bathtub spout cover		
30+	Birth announcements		
30+	Thank-you notes		
1	Growth chart		
1	CD or DVD player and soft music or "white noise" (all sound frequencies)		
	page subtotal		$
	first page subtotal		$
	second page subtotal		$
	third page subtotal		$
	fourth page subtotal		$
	Grand Total		$

Risks During Pregnancy

CHAPTER 12 • Parenthood

Practice	Increased Risk	Result
Smoking/exposure to secondhand smoke	Stillbirth Sudden Infant Death Syndrome (SIDS) Low birth weight	Unexpected death of the infant during sleep
Drinking alcoholic beverages	Miscarriage (spontaneous abortion) Fetal Alcohol Syndrome (FAS) Alcohol-Related Birth Defects (ARBD)	Birth defects that include facial anomalies, growth retardation, and neural abnormalities (impaired learning skills, memory, judgment, hearing, coordination, impulse control, attention, social skills, etc.) Congenital defects (malformations occurring prior to birth) of the heart, bone, kidney, vision, or hearing
Drug usage (non-prescription, prescription, herbal, and excess nutrient supplementation)	Impaired fetal growth and development	Birth defects; damage to the central nervous system promoting abnormal sleep, crying, and behavior; reduced ability to learn; being either hypersensitive or withdrawn; becoming addicted to the substance, resulting in withdrawal after birth
Painting, cleaning, and using strong chemicals in daily life *Getting x-rayed by the physician or dentist*	Exposure to lead, mercury, heavy metals, pesticides, epoxies, solders, paints, stains, ionizing radiation, x-rays, aromatic hydrocarbons (gasoline, turpentine, model glue, mothballs, etc.), organic solvents (acetone, xylene, etc.), and hazardous gases	Miscarriage Inhibited ability to learn and damage to the developing nervous system Low birth weight Malformation of the fetus
Contact with the parasite Toxoplasma gondii *Coming in contact with cat feces (emptying cat litter trays, gardening in contaminated soil, etc.)* *Eating infected meat that has not been cooked thoroughly*	*Toxoplasmosis* (400–4,000 congenital cases yearly with 750 deaths, of which 375 were caused by eating contaminated meat) Miscarriage, stillbirth	90% appear normal at birth, but problems arise in the future (55–80% future incidence) Eye infections, severely impaired sight, or blindness Enlarged liver and spleen, jaundice, epilepsy, cerebral palsy, learning disabilities, mental retardation

Risks During Pregnancy, cont.

CHAPTER 12 • Parenthood

Practice	Increased Risk	Result
Promiscuous living *Using contaminated needles when engaging in intravenous drug use* *Transfer of human fluids*	STDs/AIDS Mother with HIV has 20–50% risk of passing it to baby; mother with active AIDS has 60–70% risk.	There were 3.1 million AIDS-related deaths worldwide (including 610,000 children under the age of 15) in 2002 (UNAIDS. *AIDS Epidemic Update,* December, 2002). AIDS is the fifth leading cause of death in the United States for people aged 25–44 (Deaths: Final Data for 2000. National Vital Statistics Reports; Vol. 50, no. 15. Hyattsville, Maryland: National Center for Health Statistics, 2002). Active herpes (HSV-2) can be life-threatening to a newborn; a C-section is often done. Infants with AIDS usually die before the age of 2.
Rhesus negative (Rh-) mother carrying a child fathered by an Rh positive (Rh+) man	Rh incompatibility (the mother's body develops antibodies against the Rh+ substances)	Infant anemia, severe jaundice, heart failure, or brain damage unless the physicians administer Rh immune globulin (RhIg) to prevent the mother from developing high levels of antibodies. (The mother and child may also require an in utero blood transfusion.)
Low-carbohydrate diets	Deprivation of glucose for the fetal brain	Impairment of child's ability to learn and think

Sexually Transmitted Diseases

CHAPTER 12 • Parenthood

Sexually Transmitted Diseases

Sexually transmitted diseases (STDs) are diseases and infections transmitted by the exchange of body fluids or skin contamination during sexual activity.
Only about half of the more than fifteen STDs are charted here. One out of five Americans has an STD; two-thirds of all STDs occur in persons younger than twenty-five.

Disease	Information	Consequences
Syphilis (Fewer than 40,000 cases per year in the U.S.)	Caused by a spiral-shaped bacterium *Treponema pallidum* Stages include 1. Primary 2. Secondary 3. Latent 4. Late	Presence of syphilis increases the risk of getting HIV 1. 10–90 days after exposure, a painless sore (chancre) or many sores appear, then heal in 3–6 weeks 2. Rashes (on various parts of the body and of varying types), sore throat, swollen lymph glands, fever, fatigue, and headaches occur; highly infectious during first two stages (which usually last about 2 years) 3. No outward signs visible, but disease continues to thrive 4. Paralysis; numbness; gradual blindness; heart, brain, and nerve damage; dementia; and death
Gonorrhea (Approximately 650,000 cases per year in the U.S.)	Caused by the bacterium *Neisseria gonorrhoeae*	Inflammation of mucous lining of the genital tract and urethra producing infectious drainage; if untreated, may result in **sterility** (the inability to reproduce) Increased risk of PID in women
PID (Pelvic Inflammatory Disease) (Approximately 1 million women per year)	Infection of the internal reproductive organs in women resulting from other STDs 15% of all infertility in women in the U.S. due to PID resulting from an untreated STD	Permanent damage to the fallopian tubes and reproductive tissues Can lead to infertility (due to scar tissue blocking the path of the ovum), ectopic pregnancy (fertilized egg grows in the fallopian tube or location other than the uterus), and chronic pelvic pain Symptoms include fever, unusual discharge, and pain
Trichomoniasis (Approximately 5 million cases per year)	Caused by a single-celled protozoan, *Trichomonas vaginalis*	Discharge with odor, discomfort, itching, and occasionally lower abdominal pain Premature delivery in pregnant women Increased risk of acquiring HIV if exposed

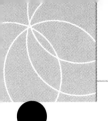

Sexually Transmitted Diseases, cont.

CHAPTER 12 • Parenthood

Sexually Transmitted Diseases		
Disease	**Information**	**Consequences**
Chlamydia (Approximately 3 million cases per year in the U.S.)	Caused by the bacterium *Chlamydia trachomatis* Is the most frequently reported STD in the U.S. Teenage girls have highest rate of infection	75% of women and 50% of men without any symptoms Increased risk of acquiring HIV 40% of women at risk for PID
HIV/AIDS (Acquired Immune Deficiency Syndrome) (Approximately 40 million people infected worldwide—1 in every 100 around the world)	An estimated 40,000 new HIV infections in the U.S. per year; 850,000–950,000 living with it—¼ not aware they have it Also contracted by intravenous drug use (contaminated needles), contaminated transfusions, birth when the mother is infected, any direct transfer of human fluids to an open sore or cut	Lowered immunity leaves the body open to opportunistic infections (normal microorganisms—bacteria, fungi, etc.—increase without restraint, causing an outbreak of disease), which can lead to death Infections include oral thrush, pneumonia, blisters, tuberculosis, meningitis, and cancer (Kaposi's sarcoma) Having other STDs makes a person 2 to 5 times more likely to acquire HIV
Genital HPV (Human Papillomavirus) (Approximately 20 million people infected; 5.5 million get a new infection each year)	Caused by the human papillomavirus (HPV), a group of more than 100 types, of which over 30 are sexually transmitted No cure for HPV	Virus lives in the skin or mucus membranes and does not always cause symptoms Genital warts possible weeks or months after contamination Ten types of HPV associated with the development of cervical cancer in women
Genital Herpes (Approximately 45 million in the U.S.; 1 out of 5 teens and adults infected with HSV-2)	Caused by the Herpes Simplex Virus type 1 (HSV-1) or type 2 (HSV-2) HSV-2 infection more common in women No cure for Herpes	HSV-1 spread by the saliva and causes sores on the mouth and lips HSV-2 yields either mild symptoms or painful genital sores, fever, swollen glands Potentially fatal infection can be spread to the baby of a mother with HSV-2 Increased susceptibility to HIV infection

APGAR Scoring

CHAPTER 12 • Parenthood

Apgar Scoring

In 1952, Virginia Apgar, a physician, published the following way of discerning whether a baby is in distress. If the child scores fewer than 7 points, the infant will be assisted and closely monitored.

Sign	0 Points	1 Point	2 Points
Activity (muscle tone)	Limp (weak or no activity)	Some movement of arms and legs	Active motion
Pulse (heartbeat)	Not detectable	Below 100 bpm*	Above 100 bpm
Grimace (reaction when soles of feet are flicked)	No response to stimulation	Grimace	Sneezes, coughs, or gives lusty cry
Appearance (skin color)	Pale or blue-gray	Body pink and extremities blue	Completely pink
Respiration	Absent	Weak, irregular cry	Good, strong cry

*bpm = beats per minute

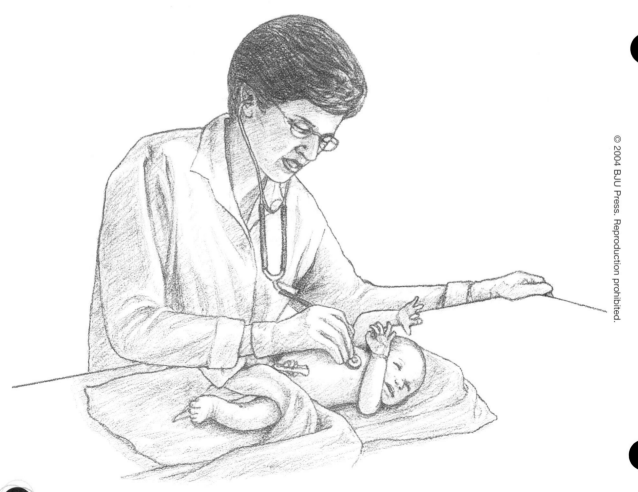

Case Studies

Read the following case studies and identify which type of adoption each case typifies.

closed adoption

cooperative adoption

foster care adoption

independent adoption

international adoption

open adoption

private agency adoption

semi-open adoption

traditional adoption

transracial adoption

1. Jonathan and Leigh could hardly believe that they were on their way to the Ukraine. They realized that the legal work and final approval of the government would need to be hurdled. However, their dream of having a daughter was almost fulfilled. "Sara Beth," Lord willing, would soon be a part of their family.

2. Lance's parents were both young teenagers who had never expected to have a baby. Dreams of high-school diplomas, college, and careers seemed lost. However, during her pregnancy, Lance's mother was saved. Lisë, the lady who was discipling her, and Lisë's husband, Armand, were childless. Financially, they could never have afforded normal adoption fees. But Lance's parents asked if Armand and Lisë would consider adopting the baby when he was born. So Lance was reared in a Christian home with parents who wanted and loved him. His birth parents had gone their separate ways, but Lance knew who they were. As he was growing up, they were family friends who would drop by occasionally. Dad Armand and Mom Lisë kept in contact with them and updated them with letters and photos.

3. Jung did not know who his birth parents were. The adoption agency took care of all communications. He did know that they were accessible in case of an emergency (need for transplants, genetic history, or family medical history). He also knew that they cared about him and wanted to know about him. The adoption agency regularly sent his pictures, copies of school report cards, and summaries of his development to his birth parents. Jung did not know whether they were citizens of America or Korea. All he knew was that his parents by adoption loved him; and at a distance, his birth parents loved him in their own way.

4. Lucinda felt safe at last. She was so young, alone, and afraid. The people at Home Adoption Agency were Christians interested in placing her baby in a Christian home. She knew that she was totally incapable of keeping the baby. However, she also knew that having an abortion would be wrong. The workers at Home Adoption would take care of finding a home for her baby and filing the necessary legal work and would support her during her pregnancy and delivery. She had asked the Lord to forgive her for her sins and was doing her best to seek a solution that would be best for the baby. She could rest now, and she even felt that she was, in a sense, at home.

Case Studies, cont.

CHAPTER 12 • Parenthood

5. Elliot and his three sisters last saw his parents as the police took them away for their third offence of drug trafficking. His parents would never be out of prison in time to rear their family even if the courts would allow them to bring up their children. The assigned foster parents were Christians and insisted that Elliot and his sisters attend church. Elliot found the peace, stability, and love he longed for when he accepted Christ as his Savior. Now another miracle had occurred. The Christian couple had offered to adopt all of them!

6. Celeste and Ian bravely faced the new responsibilities of parenthood. The infant was so small, so wanted, so loved. As new parents, they knew that this baby would be more than a child born in America and reared in America; he would be a Christian American reared to love God and country. Celeste and Ian knew that their baby's parents would remain anonymous to them. In turn, their privacy was also protected in that the birth parents would not know who or where they were.

7. Although Braden and Moriah were not Asian, they did not hesitate when the opportunity to adopt a baby girl from China came. They looked at the adoption as an answer to their prayers. They had always wanted children but, due to Moriah's health, knew they would never be birth parents. Besides, this provided an opportunity for them to rear a child for the Lord.

8. Cassie knew that she had only a few hours to live. Immorality, drug abuse, and alcohol had been her way of life. Now she fought through the haze of medication and pain to make amends. She finally prayed the sinner's prayer that she had avoided all her life. Her Christian parents, who had loved her in spite of her rebellious nature and lifestyle, held her hands and cried. Through parched lips she requested that they adopt her daughter, Traci. Their family friend, an attorney, was there to witness her request. Traci was already fatherless, but upon Cassie's death, she would be an orphan.

9. Malia and David thoroughly understood and appreciated the terms of the adoption. Little Judah would be totally theirs to rear. However, they willingly signed the contract that committed them to inform the birth parents in case of a health emergency involving Judah, as well as his graduation from school and his marriage.

10. Zach did not know how to contact his birth parents. He knew that he had been adopted but never knew who his parents were or where they were from. All the records of his adoption were sealed and inaccessible. The only problem was that he now had cancer and was in need of a donor for an organ transplant.

Childcare Project

CHAPTER 13 • Infants

This project is worth 50 points. Select the activities you would like to do, but they must add up to 50 points. Fill in the lessons and principles for each and hand in pictures, tapes, and task explanations in a manila envelope attached to this page. Write your name on all inserts as well as on this paper and the envelope. The project is due on _____.

Date	Task	Ages of Children	Specific Lessons Learned/ Principles to Remember
	Feed and burp an infant 3 months of age or younger. List the method(s) of burping used. Identify the method that worked. **5 points**		
	Prepare baby food and feed it to a 4 to 10-month-old baby. Write the type of food, commercial or homemade, and how the food was warmed. Explain the baby's reaction. **5 points**		
	Diaper and dress a baby 1–12 months old. List the type of diaper and the wipe, cleanser, or ointment used. Write the type of outfit you put on the baby. **5 points**		
	Play and sing with children (1–5 years old) for 45 minutes or more. List all the songs sung. Describe the instrumental accompaniment used. **5 points**		
	Provide crayons and paper for 2–5-year-olds (one from each age) to draw a picture of a family and a house. Have them explain their pictures so you can identify people on the back of each picture. Write each child's name and age. Analyze their coordination and perception of people drawn. Place the pictures in the envelope. **5 points**		

Childcare Project, cont.

CHAPTER 13 • Infants

Date	Task	Ages of Children	Specific Lessons Learned/ Principles to Remember
	Take care of a sick child (2–5 years old). Take his temperature and give him the prescribed medicine. Prepare a snack tray for him. Read to him. Explain the child's sickness. List the medications, foods, and drinks you provided. List the books you read to him. **5 points**		
	Record communication of children in the correct age sequence (infant—age 5). Use cassette, video, or disc. Place in envelope. Be sure to identify the name and age with an analysis (cooing, babbling, etc.) for each sample. **15 points**		
	Plan, prepare, and give a party for children (between 2 and 5 years old). Include a list of the children, games, music, food, décor, and basic plans. **15 points**		

Postpartum Fatigue
CHAPTER 13 • Infants

What to Do	Specific Suggestions
Relax and rest.	Sleep when the baby sleeps; turn the phone off and the answering machine on (low volume); rest without guilt.
Keep spiritually fed.	Have personal devotions; use free moments to pray; listen to recorded messages; sing hymns and choruses to the baby; seek wisdom and see things in the light of God's Word.
Get help.	Pay for an occasional babysitter to come in while you go shopping, out for dinner with husband and friends, or hiking for a couple of hours. If income is tight, trade times with other new mothers (you watch their baby for two hours and they later watch your baby for two hours). Get assistance from "Grandma and Granddad" or other family members (church family members are often closer in relationship and distance).
Exercise.	Get up and get going! Use video or DVD workouts with free weights. Take long walks, bike rides, or hikes with an all-terrain trailer/jogger stroller. Go swimming with the baby (after your six-week checkup).
Expand your mind.	Listen to audio books; take the baby to the library and check out books to read or listen to while you do tasks or take walks.
Share and enjoy.	Get together with other moms; explore your city with babies in tow; have picnics at the park; have a Bible study with other new mothers; learn a hobby with friends.
Learn to say "no."	Reduce commitments. Review your priorities before making plans or accepting new obligations.
Work together.	Divide household chores and tasks with your husband. If there are other children in the home, divide and conquer the housework.
Keep things simple.	Use quick and simple recipes and meal plans that utilize oven meals, the crockpot, or the microwave. Organize by placing items near the places they are used (put your reading material near the rocker, the diaper stacker and disposal unit near the changing location, etc.).
Say goodbye to perfectionism.	There is no such thing as a perfect baby, a perfect mother, or a perfectly clean house. No matter how wonderful the baby is or you are, both are sinful beings and are prone to error. Be as clean and as organized as possible, but a spotless house without a maid is a fantasy.

Benefits of Breastfeeding

CHAPTER 13 • Infants

Benefits of Breastfeeding

For the Infant

- Provides for the removal of meconium (first intestinal discharges of a newborn)
- Provides all necessary nutrients
- Readily available in the right amounts and at the proper temperature
- Bacteriologically safe
- Increases favorable conditions for the growth of good bacteria
- Nutrients are easily digested and available for his use
- Provides antibodies from the mother to protect from many infections
- Decreases the risk of ear infections
- Decreases the risk of respiratory infections
- Decreases the risk of eczema, allergies, and asthma
- Improves infant's intellectual development
- Helps infant to evade many food allergies
- Lowers the risk of malocclusion and decay of primary teeth
- Changes in composition and quality as the baby ages
- May reduce future problems of obesity, hypertension, and Type 1 Diabetes (IDDM)

For the Mother

- Provides increased maternal bonding
- Helps her uterus to contract back to its normal size
- Burns up two to five hundred calories daily
- Conserves her iron stores
- Raises bone remineralization levels
- Aids in increasing the good cholesterol levels
- May serve as a deterrent against ovarian, premenopausal breast, and uterine cancer

For the Father

- Saves money (not having to purchase formula and bottle supplies)
- Usually involves less offensive dirty diapers
- Enjoys lower health-care costs
- Does not have to prepare formula and heat bottles

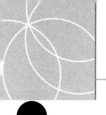

Baby Bottle Basics

CHAPTER 13 • Infants

Put the following instructions in the proper sequence by drawing straight lines connecting the answer to the sequence.

Test the formula's temperature by shaking a drop onto your inner wrist without touching the nipple.

Using clean bottles, nipples, measuring cups, mixing utensils, and can openers, measure the correct amount of formula and water.

Discard any formula left in the bottle after the baby has finished feeding and within one hour after feeding begins.

After checking the expiration date on the formula, wash the lid and shake liquid formula before opening.

Burp the baby when he has consumed half of his bottle or becomes fussy. Gently rub or pat the baby's back while holding him against your shoulder, in a sitting position on your lap, or on his tummy over your lap. Protect your clothing since he may spit up.

Wash your hands with soap and warm water.

Hold the baby and do not prop the bottle to leave the baby alone. Formula should fill the nipple up to the neck. The nipple should be held at a right angle to the baby's mouth.

Warm the bottle in a bowl of warm water or under warm running water. Do not warm formula in the microwave.

1st

2nd

3rd

4th

5th

6th

7th

8th

Introducing Solid Foods

CHAPTER 13 • Infants

Age (Months)	Developmental Skills	Foods Added
0–4	Rooting reflex (turns head toward any object that brushes against the cheek); swallows using back and later front of the tongue	Breast milk or infant formula (continue until end of 12th month)
4–6	Extrusion reflex (pushes food out with tongue) diminishes; can turn head away; indicates desire for food by leaning forward and opening mouth; can sit	Diluted iron-fortified rice cereal and other cereals (wheat last at end of 6th month); pureed vegetables (sweetest ones last)
	Palmar grasp (holds items with palm of hand); can chew on hand	Pureed fruits (sweetest ones last), finger foods (toast, teething biscuits)
6–8	Pincer grasp (holds items with finger and thumb); can voluntarily release items in hand; begins to drink from a cup	Dry, unsweetened cereal; pieces of textured vegetables and fruits; strained meats; unsweetened juice
8–10	Holds bottle; sits unsupported; recognizes container-content relationships; grabs food and spoon	Bread and cereal from the table; yogurt; soft, cooked vegetables and fruits at table; chopped meats and casseroles; pasta
10–12	Begins to have control of the spoon but spills some	Food that sticks to the spoon (cooked cereal, mashed potatoes, cottage cheese, cooked legumes), spaghetti

Daily intake: 2 servings meat, poultry, fish, eggs, or legumes; breast milk or formula for each meal and snack; 2 servings fruit; 3 servings vegetables; 4–6 servings breads and cereals at table in addition to 2–4 tbsp infant cereal (a serving is equal to ⅓–½ the size of an adult serving or 1 tbsp of vegetables, fruits, and meats)

When preparing and feeding solid foods, be sure that

- the food is fresh (seals are not broken; buttons on jar lids curve down).
- cereals are stored away from chemicals, soaps, and foods with strong odors.
- all equipment, utensils, bowls, counters, and tables are clean.
- your hands are washed.
- salt, spices, or honey are not added to infant foods. Use sugar sparingly if at all.
- skin, pits, seeds, gristle, and bones are removed from food.
- you avoid overcooking in order to preserve nutrients.
- you do not heat in a microwave since uneven heating may cause hot spots.
- you heat and serve only as much as the child will eat at one feeding. Enzymes on a spoon used by the baby will break down any starches in leftover food.
- opened jars are refrigerated immediately and used within 2–3 days.

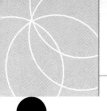

Infant Progression

CHAPTER 13 • Infants

Physical Development	
The baby grows in height, weight, and motor skills. His senses become more refined and his movements more purposeful.	Reflexive reactions (automatic response to stimulus). Moro reflex (infant arches back, extends arms when startled or if support lessens). Rooting (stroke on cheek results in baby turning). Sucking (item placed in infant's mouth will initiate sucking). Babinski (infant's toes fan out when sole of foot is stroked). Palmar grasp (involuntary grip when palm is touched). Rolls over and sits without support (7 mo.). Ulnar grasp—prereaching and grasping items in palm (4 mo.). Pincer grasp—picking items up with finger and thumb (9 mo.). Coordinated grasp and release motions (10–12 mo.). Crawls (7 mo.), pulls up to vertical position (8 mo.), stands (11 mo.), takes steps and walks (12 mo.).

Mental Development	
The basics of speech and communication are established as he learns to say what he hears (incorporating the language, tones, and emphasis he heard).	Recognizes mother's voice (first week). Cries, sucks, and clicks his tongue. Coos (makes non-crying sounds) and babbles (makes repetitive consonant and vowel combinations). Accidentally imitates a sound—lallation. Intentionally imitates a sound—echolalia. Holophrases (uses single-word expressions of the entire situation). Understands simple parental commands.

Social Development	
The child is totally dependent on his parents but is oblivious to the stress of his demands for attention.	Smile develops from reflex (birth) to selective social (2 mo.) to smile of pleasure (3 mo.) to laughter (4 mo.). Responds favorably to people; is outgoing. Recognizes mother and makes eye contact (2 mo.). Fusses when familiar people leave. Objects to strangers and can show fear. Is suspicious of strangers (7 mo.). Extends toy to another person but will not release it. Enjoys being read to and playing patty-cake and peekaboo.

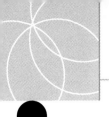

Toddler Progression

CHAPTER 14 • Toddlers

Stature

Physical Development

The changes of a toddler are less drastic in growth but major in fine-tuning his abilities.

- Grows less quickly after his first birthday (has grown about half his birth length). His head and abdomen are large in proportion to his short legs and arms.
- Walks with wide gait and uses arms for balance. Walks forward, backward, and, eventually, up steps with help.
- Runs, jumps, squats, climbs up and down furniture, carries several items while walking, stands on tiptoes, and kicks a ball by age two.

Wisdom

Mental Development

Bridges are built between a child's thoughts and his ability to express them. Gestures turn to words and questions are answered. Talking, reading to him, listening, identifying items, and not using "baby talk" responses help him to learn. Do not depend on television, computer games, or toys to provide interaction. Give simple, clear instructions.

- Begins to associate words with objects.
- Likes to pretend and engage in make-believe play.
- Understands more than he can say. Repeats words you say.
- Will say *hi, bye, please,* and *thank you* when prompted.
- Responds to questions by pointing ("Where is your nose?").
- Uses telegraphic speech—simple sentences of one or two words ("All gone." "Mama here."). Uses pivot words such as *go, my,* or *more* ("Daddy go." "My dog." "More play.").
- Substitutes "me" for "I" ("Me sleep." "Me want dolly.").
- Two often-used words are "Why?" and "No!"
- Begins using words with plural and past tense. ("One man, two mans." "He goed home." "She holded the dogses.")
- Adds words to vocabulary (500–1,000 words).

Favor with God

Spiritual Development

A toddler has an aptitude for the things of God. Pictures and Bible stories, simple verses, fingerplays. hymns, and praying develop respect for and awareness of God.

- Is able to comprehend basic spiritual truths.
  1. God made all things. God made me.
  2. God loves me.
  3. God listens when I pray.
  4. God sees me all the time.
  5. God can do all things.
- Can learn to close eyes, bow head, and fold hands for prayer.

Favor with Man

Social Development

The child passes from a state of complete dependence at infancy to a surge of independence at 18 months.

- Often fluctuates between fierce independence and clinging. May exhibit shyness.
- Imitates simple actions, shows his toy, and will take turns.
- Empathetic to others who are upset or crying.
- Likes to tease.
- Egocentric; notices people only in relation to himself.
- Loves to imitate others (especially adults mowing, vacuuming, shopping, cooking, etc.).
- Can be contrary and controlling; can be contrite.
- Demonstrates complete selfishness; will not share. Plays by himself within a group (parallel play).
- Becomes upset by mother's absence (separation anxiety).

Suggested Toys

CHAPTER 14 • Toddlers

Development	1 year	2 years	3 years	4 years	5 years
Motor skills	Riding toys, push-pull toys, balls, bath toys, activity walkers	Large waffle blocks, block trains, boxes, low slides, bubbles	Playground equipment, tricycles, cars, trucks, planes	Swimming, rope ladders, dolls with buttons and zippers	Skates, bicycle with training wheels, see-saw
Creative play	Large stackable blocks and plastic snap-together toys	Water play in sink, large crayons, sandbox, wood blocks	Finger-paint, sidewalk chalk, clay, yarn drawing on carpet, large beads and string	Blackboard and chalk, sewing cards, hard plastic snap and stack blocks	Pencil, paper, folds, cutting, paste, poster paint, finger puppets, blanket and chairs
Intellectual skills	Nesting and stacking toys, sound-making toys	Peg puzzles, large plastic clock, simple musical toys, quiet books	Children's musical toys, letter and number toys	Puzzles, electronic reading/ writing programs, animal and insect investigations	Books, magnifying glass, magnets, plants and seeds
Dramatic play	Stuffed animals, soft play farms or house items	Telephone, dolls, pretend house items, large boxes	Hats, dress-ups	Dress-ups, playhouse, dollhouse	Play-store items, occupational toys, tents

Choking Hazards

CHAPTER 14 • Toddlers

Potential Causes of Choking in Children
Nuts, sunflower seeds, pumpkin seeds, etc.
Raw vegetables such as celery, carrots, and peas; whole olives; cherry tomatoes
Hard candy, lollipops, and cough drops; taffy; marshmallows; caramels and jellybeans
Popcorn
Raw, unpeeled fruit slices, such as apples and pears; whole grapes; cherries with pits; dried fruits such as raisins and apricots
Chunks of food, especially meat or poultry; hot dogs or sausages served whole or cut in "coins"; cheese cubes
Spoonfuls of peanut butter
Snack chips
Coins, button-cell batteries
Buttons (loose as well as those attached to clothing)
Deflated or broken latex ballons
Pencils, crayons, and erasers; pen and marker caps
Rings, earrings
Nails, screws, staples, safety pins, tacks, etc.
Small toys, such as tiny figures, balls, marbles, or toys with small parts
Holiday decorations, including tinsel
Small rocks
Damaged or loose nipples on pacifiers or bottles

Food Items is the label for the top portion of the table; *Non-Food Items* is the label for the bottom portion.

Used by permission of the International Food Information Council. ("Choking and Kids: Prevention Is the Key," *Food Insight* January/February 2002, p. 3)

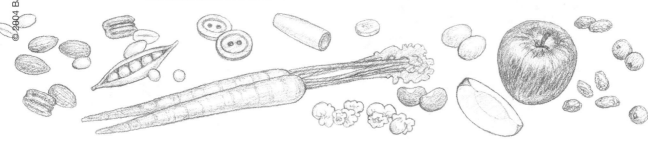

Toxic Products

CHAPTER 14 • Toddlers

Cherry tree twig

Bird of paradise

Toxic Plants

Amaryllis bulbs	Daffodil bulbs	Jerusalem cherry	Philodendron
Angel's trumpet	Daphne	Jimson weed (thorn apple)	Poinsettia
Antheriums	Delphinium	Jonquil bulbs	Poison hemlock
Autumn crocus	Dieffenbachia	Lantana	Pokeweed stems & roots
Azaleas	Elderberry	Larkspur	Privet
Bird of paradise	Elephant's ear	Lilies	Rattlebox
Bittersweet seeds	English ivy	Lily-of-the-valley	Rhododendron
Bleeding heart	Foxglove (Digitalis)	Mistletoe berries	Rhubarb leaves
Bloodroot	Holly berries	Morning glory	Sweet pea seeds
Buttercups	Hyacinth bulbs	Mountain laurel	Tansy leaves & flowers
Caladium	Hydrangea bulbs & leaves	Narcissus bulbs	Tulip bulbs
Castor beans	Iris	Nightshade	Wisteria seeds & pods
Cherry tree twigs and leaves	Jack-in-the-pulpit	Oleander	Yew
Chrysanthemums	Jasmine	Pecan tree leaves	

Toxic Chemicals

ammonia	dishwasher cleaners	iodine	perfume
aspirin	disinfectants	kerosene	pine oil
bleach	drain cleaners	lamp oil	rust remover
cologne	fuel	lighter fluid	shaving cream
cosmetics	gasoline	lotion	toilet bowl cleaner
deodorizers	glue	motor oil	turpentine
detergents	insecticides	naphtha	water softener

Poinsettia

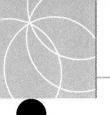

Proverbs of Discipline

CHAPTER 14 • Toddlers

Why is discipline necessary? Match each of the following phrases to the verses from the book of Proverbs. Write the descriptive phrase on the lines provided.

To bring all (but the scorner who gains nothing) closer to insightful perception

To elevate honor and success through controlled conduct

To obey God's command to mold a child's character early in life

To promote submission to parents and God (preventing wickedness, premature death, and hell)

To direct a child away from unwise influences and toward godly instruction

To show parental love

To suppress moral immaturity and the innate bent for folly (wisdom leads to life; folly leads to death)

1. "Poverty and shame shall be to him that refuseth instruction: but he that regardeth reproof shall be honoured." (13:18)

   _____

   _____

2. "He that spareth his rod hateth his son: but he that loveth him chasteneth him betimes." (13:24)

   _____

   _____

3. "Chasten thy son while there is hope, and let not thy soul spare for his crying." (19:18)

   _____

   _____

4. "Smite a scorner, and the simple will beware: and reprove one that hath understanding, and he will understand knowledge." (19:25)

   _____

   _____

5. "Cease, my son, to hear the instruction that causeth to err from the words of knowledge." (19:27)

   _____

   _____

Proverbs of Discipline, cont.

CHAPTER 14 • Toddlers

6. "Foolishness is bound in the heart of a child; but the rod of correction shall drive it far from him." (22:15)

_____

_____

7. "Withhold not correction from the child: for if thou beatest him with the rod, he shall not die. Thou shalt beat him with the rod, and shalt deliver his soul from hell." (23:13–14)

_____

_____

Contractual Agreements

CHAPTER 14 • Toddlers

Many schools and homes have found that cowriting an agreement between the child and the authority figure helps to bring about desired results without conflict. For instance, in the home, the child (usually aged four through high school) can see the expectations of his parents, his time limits, and his rewards (privileges, bonuses, etc.). The child also learns to be responsible and learns to understand that there are consequences. The parents benefit since they no longer have to remind the child endlessly about chores and listen to whining, promises of "in a minute," or accusations of "you didn't tell me." This behavior contract may take a bit of time and communication to initiate, but it is worthwhile.

Read the following contract for a preschooler. Using it as a guide, construct a similar contract between you and your parents for weekly chores for three weeks. At the end of the time period, complete the assessment form and hand the page in to your teacher. This project is due on _____.

Preschool Example

This is a contract between _____ and _____.
It is understood that said child will fulfill the following:
1. Do all tasks without complaining, arguing, or being reminded.
2. Make his bed correctly in the morning before breakfast.
3. Brush his teeth thoroughly before leaving the house (for school, play, church, etc.), when arriving home (after snacks), and before bedtime at night, flossing before the bedtime brushing.
4. Feed and water the pets before leaving for school or church.
5. Put all toys and clothes neatly in their proper places before going to bed at night.
6. Empty all the bedroom trashcans into the large outdoor can (locking the cover) and return the cans to the proper places and rooms. This will be done once a week on _____ before bedtime.

It is understood that if the tasks listed above are not completed on time or in the manner described, the following will occur:
1. Loss of play time, phone time, and visitation with friends until the task is completed as described above. In addition, there will be a 24-hour loss of television and electronic game time.
2. Three infractions within the week will result in $_____ less allowance.

However, if the child completes all tasks given in this contract as agreed, a bonus of _____ shall be given on Saturday before bedtime.

Signed: _____   Date: _____

_____

_____

Contractual Agreements, cont.

CHAPTER 14 • Toddlers

Home and Family Contract

This is a temporary contract between _____ and _____. Because it is a class assignment, this will be binding for the time between _____ and _____. It is understood that said teenager will perform the following:

1. _____.

2. _____.

3. _____.

4. _____.

5. _____.

6. _____.

It is understood that if the tasks listed above are not completed on time or in the manner described, the following will occur:

1. _____.

2. _____.

However, if the teenager completes all tasks given in this contract as agreed, a bonus of _____ shall be given on Saturday before bedtime.

Signed: _____   Date: _____

_____

_____

Assessment

1. During this project, I had to face negative consequences _____ times.
2. I obtained the bonus _____ times.
3. I found that this contract project _____.
4. My parents' reactions indicated _____.
5. Improvements to the contract would include _____ _____.

Because

Do you remember hearing people give reasons for directives? When a preschooler hears a directive ("Do this." "Do that."), the initial response is usually, "Why?" Many parents respond by saying "Because I said to."

However, rules and directives should be based on principles that are larger than the parent, firmer than the directive, and longer lasting than a lifetime.

Consider the following directives and write the biblical principle addressed. Then, using a concordance, write out a verse and reference identifying the biblical principle to be applied.

Come here!

Principle: Obedience
Verse:

Do not say bad words.

Principle: Control of the tongue
Verse:

Help your brother.

Principle: Be helpful.
Verse:

Listen to me.

Principle: Wisdom of parents
Verse:

Do not hit or bite.

Principle: Be kind.
Verse:

Quit whining.

Principle: Be grateful.
Verse:

Quiet Activity Box

CHAPTER 15 • Preschoolers

You may use the following ideas to create your own Quiet Activity box for preschoolers. These boxes may be given to nephews, nieces, neighbors, or friends, or produced as a youth activity for missionaries or church outreach gifts. Because some of the project requires sewing, much of it requires cutting, and a lot of it requires detailing, it is best done in multiples (i.e., while one person does all the cutting of the felt spots for the ladybug, another person can sew the zipper in the red felt background). If 6–10 boxes are done at a time with several people doing one specific side or job, the boxes come together rather quickly.

Please note that sturdy fabric should be used for the base and that sides must be sewn with right sides together around the edges with the last sides left open for turning. Thin quilt batting should be sewn with the side layers to provide stability and flat cushioning. To personalize a box, a child's name can simply be written on with a fabric or permanent marker. Anyone using permanent or fabric markers should also make sure that the fabric on which they will be writing does not leak through or bleed around the edges of the design (practice on a scrap piece first and place it on layers of protective paper until dry). Before sewing the last box ends together, stuff the box with pillow stuffing. Then hand-stitch the box sides closed.

1. **Anchor strong string on top and bottom. Use beads large enough not to cause choking.**

2. **Sew zipper into red felt covered with felt black spots. Place wordless book inside.**

3. **Attach felt shapes. Use velcro dots and yarn as the strings. Trace the smaller shapes above yarn ends using fabric ink pens.**

4. **Cut a circle from clear acrylic (overhead transparency). Place over felt sun with clock-face numbers written in fabric ink pen. Anchor cardboard hands in place with buttons in the center holes at the end of the hands.**

5. **Weave a shoelace in the felt shoe. Use grommets to secure the opening so that the laces will slide through easily.**

6. **Either attach a real mitten or make one with felt. Draw a face on it.**

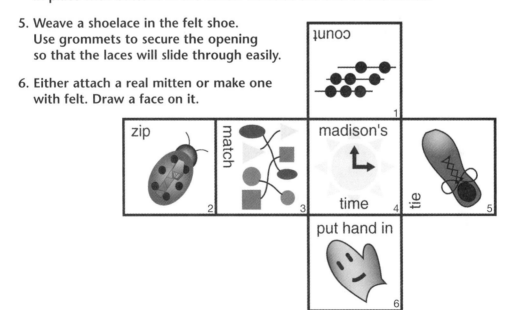

Preschooler Progression

CHAPTER 15 • Preschoolers

Stature

Physical Development *Skills are honed and movements develop fluidity. Little by little, control is gained over actions: gross motor skills and fine motor skills.*	• Can easily run, climb, use alternating feet up the stairs, and ride a tricycle. Fine motor skills improve, so he can turn pages one at a time, make varied strokes with a crayon, turn rotating handles, and manipulate puzzles and building games well. • Can come down the stairs using alternating feet, gallop, and hop with one foot by about the age of four. Fine motor skills are displayed in ability to cut on lines, dress self and use buttons, and trace simple shapes. • Perfects technical skills of tying shoelaces, skating, skipping, jumping rope, and gymnastic feats by age six. His fine motor skills include printing letters and his name, using pencils and scissors smoothly, building complex block structures, and solving simple puzzles.

Wisdom

Mental Development *Cognition (processes in which one develops awareness, knowledge, and reasoning abilities) expands and becomes fine-tuned. Speech capabilities are sometimes hindered by inability to say certain sounds.*	• Expands sentences ("They was so loud." "I am three years old!"). • Enjoys word play ("tutti-fruity," "fancy-wansy," etc.). Coins a word if he needs a word and does not know it. • Can count, can identify an abundance of animals, has increased words and added capability of following more grammatical rules. • Can follow two-step directives, tell a story, categorize items, use descriptors, and provide explanations. • Is very imaginative and creative.

Favor with God

Spiritual Development
 	
A preschooler knows the difference between right and wrong. He feels guilt when he is bad. His moral behavior and spiritual awareness hinge greatly on daily Bible application in the home. Until he is saved, parents can guide him in the way he should go, but he will not have the Spirit's leading.
	• Has increasing ability to sit still for prayer and church.
	• Can be trained to be kind, obedient, etc.
	• Should be taught basic biblical principles (catechism) that may be used by God to lead him to salvation.
	  1. God made me and all things.
	  2. Jesus is God's Son.
	  3. God sent Jesus to show His love for me.
	  4. The Bible is God's Word.
	  5. The Bible tells me about God, the world, and people God made.
	  6. The Bible tells me to obey God, my parents, and my teachers.

Favor with Man

Social Development *Preschoolers are filled with effusive praise and spontaneous activity. Newfound communication skills and empathetic feelings allow them to adapt to social situations (more harmonious and mature around older children; more compassionate and easier paced around slow learners).*	• Can learn to share with a few others. • Begins associative play (playing separately but sharing toys or commenting on each other's behavior). • Is increasingly able to share and communicate. Engages in cooperative play (interaction and communication with other children in attaining a common goal). • Is likely to engage in short-term friendships that are quickly begun and easily ended (when interaction starts and ceases). • Spontaneously reacts with affection to family and friends. • Begins to understand causes and consequences.

Babysitting Rules

CHAPTER 15 • Preschoolers

Finish the acrostic. Find other words to form sentence reminders of basic rules that a babysitter should incorporate when he or she goes "to work." The first one is done for you.

Be on time.

_____ parental expectations.

_____ handle emergencies.

_____ visitors,

phone calls, or homework to work on.

Stay _____

_____ .

_____ emergency numbers before

parents leave.

Talk _____

_____ .

_____

play with the child.

Inspire the child _____

_____ .

Never sleep _____ .

_____ only daytime jobs until you have experience.

Name

Ready for School
CHAPTER 15 • Preschoolers

School Preparation

Help prepare a child for school by encouraging him to
• Name colors of everyday items.
• Dress himself and button and zip garments.
• Put shoes on correct feet.
• Count out silverware and plates as he sets the table.
• Help sort and fold laundry.
• Sort and count silver before washing dishes.
• Recognize his name when it is printed.
• Identify everyday objects.
• Use a variety of vocabulary words for description
• Play with other children.
• Be polite and friendly.

Childcare Considerations

CHAPTER 15 • Preschoolers

	Staff	Facilities	Program
Quality	Training? Experience? Understanding of child development? Christian? Loving and nurturing staff? Not just a job, but a ministry? Listen to and interact with children?	Licensed? Clean (open areas, refrigerator, bathrooms)? Safe? Comfortable? Posted schedule? Age-appropriate toys? Outdoor equipment? Organization? Display of children's work? Music?	Promotion of Christian philosophy? Enjoyable, happy, and positive implementation? Both small-group and individual activities? Life skills (hand washing, manners, etc.) taught?
Number	How many children assigned to each staff member? Help available? Administrators and office staff?	Number of children enrolled? Space available for children to move, play, or retreat if desired? Place for child's personal items?	Planned schedule with a variety of fun but educational activities? Time allotted for children to rest, read, or be still if desired?
Availability	Ease of contact and open communication? Parents welcomed to visit anytime?	Location close to work or home? Hours and days meet parental needs?	Encouragement of both gifted and challenged students? Summer?
Communication	Staff get down and talk to the child? Use of words that child understands? No use of baby talk?	Internet site? Telephone accessible?	Directions given clearly, kindly, and enthusiastically? Are children happy, expressive, etc.?
Cost	Contentment? Supplies furnished or made or given by teacher?	Comparable to services? Written copies of policies, fees, services, refunds?	Additional fees for art, crafts, field trips, treats, special events?
Meals	Staff supervised? Qualified meal planner? Nutrient-dense but creative and delicious foods prepared?	Preparation areas clean? Food storage area well ventilated? No trace of insects? Meal schedule available?	Meet standards of a childcare food program? Provision of breakfast, lunch, and/or dinner? Snacks?
Illness/Sick Child	Qualified attendant for sick child? Help available to tend to sick child?	Place for sick child? Toys regularly sterilized?	Activities available for sick or recuperating child? Policies for prevention of exposure?
Safety	Number of staff first-aid and CPR certified? Nurse or certified EMT available or close by?	Location and presence of fire and CO alarms? Fire hydrants? Covered outlets? Cupboard locks?	Regular fire or natural emergency drills? Security checks on people taking child out?
Equipment	Staff well versed in use and care of toys, equipment, etc.?	Safe equipment and area surrounding it? Variety?	Routine checks for problems, stability, and safety hazards?

Financial Principles

CHAPTER 16 • Financial Management

Work Ethic

Ephesians 6:6 "Not with eyeservice, as menpleasers; but as the servants of Christ, doing the will of God from the heart."
Colossians 3:22 "Servants, obey in all things your masters according to the flesh; not with eyeservice, as menpleasers; but in singleness of heart, fearing God."

- Be on time.
- Work your required time enthusiastically.
- Work hard whether or not the boss is in.
- Improve your skills.
- Look for ways to improve your time, energy, and resource management.

Budgeting Basics

- Decide on the time period of the budget.
- Establish financial goals.
- Determine sources of income.
- Estimate expenses for this time period.

A financial plan should be
- comprehensive.
- realistic.
- flexible.
- simple.

Financial Goals

CHAPTER 16 • Financial Management

1. Use the following table to list your short-term and long-term goals.

Short-Term Purchase	Date to Purchase	Approximate Cost

Long-Term Purchase	Date to Purchase	Approximate Cost

2. List specific ways to meet your goals. Make sure your plans are specific and real.

3. What factors have influenced you to set these goals?

Income and Expense Record

CHAPTER 16 • Financial Management

Record your income and expenses for one month. Evaluate your spending and saving practices. Turn in this record with a written evaluation detailing what you did well and what you could improve.

Income	January	February	March
Net Pay: Earnings			
Allowance			
Balance from previous month			
Interest/Dividends			
Monetary Gifts			
Sale of Possessions:			
Other:			
TOTAL INCOME			
Fixed Expenses			
Tithes/Offerings			
Savings			
Installment Payments:			
Insurance:			
Other:			
Flexible Expenses			
Food/Snacks			
Youth Group Activities			
School Supplies			
Clothing Purchase/Upkeep			
Personal Care:			
Recreation/Entertainment			
Transportation/Gasoline			
Other:			
TOTAL EXPENSES			
Total Income			
Total Expenses			
Balance (subtract expenses from income)			

Budget Percentage Sheet

CHAPTER 16 • Financial Management

Salary for Guideline = $_____/year

Gross Income per Month			$ _____
Category	**% Guidelines***	**Gross Income**	**Allotted Amount**
Tithe	10% of Gross	( )	= $ _____
Tax	15% of Gross	( )	= $ _____
Net Spendable Income			
Housing/Utilities**	28% of Net	( )	= $ _____
Food	15% of Net	( )	= $ _____
Auto/Transportation	12% of Net	( )	= $ _____
School/Child Care	10% of Net	( )	= $ _____
Insurance	5% of Net	( )	= $ _____
Clothing	5% of Net	( )	= $ _____
Savings	5% of Net	( )	= $ _____
Medical	5% of Net	( )	= $ _____
Recreation/Entertainment	5% of Net	( )	= $ _____
Savings/Investments	5% of Net	( )	= $ _____
Miscellaneous	5% of Net	( )	= $ _____
Total *(should not exceed your net spendable income)*			

*Guideline percentages will vary according to the amount of income and number of categories.

**It is suggested that housing, food, and transportation costs not exceed 65% of net costs.

Budget Control Sheet

CHAPTER 16 • Financial Management

Gross Income		January	February	March
Gross Pay:				
Salary				
Wages				
Commission				
Interest				
Dividends				
Previous Balance				
Other				
TOTAL INCOME				

Withholdings	Budgeted	Actual Expenses		
Federal Tax				
Social Security				
State/City Tax				
Insurance:				
Unemployment				
Health				
Life				
Other				
TOTAL WITHHELD				

Expenses	Budgeted	Actual Expenses		
Contributions:				
Tithes*				
Offerings				
Reserves:				
Savings*				
Investments				
Housing:				
Mortgage/Rent*				
Utilities: Electricity*				
Utilities: Gas/Oil*				
Utilities: Water*				
Utilities: Sanitation*				
Utilities: Telephone*				
Utilities: Other				
Food:				
Groceries				
Snacks/Vending				
Lunch Tickets				

* = Fixed Expenses

Budget Control Sheet, cont.
CHAPTER 16 • Financial Management

Expenses	Budgeted	Actual Expenses		
Transportation:				
Payments*				
Gas/Oil				
Insurance*				
License*				
Taxes*				
Maintenance/Repair				
Insurance:				
Health Insurance**				
Life Insurance**				
Other				
Clothing:				
Acquisitions				
Repairs				
Cleaning				
Medical Expenses:				
Physician				
Dentist				
Pharmaceuticals				
Other				
Debts:				
Credit Card				
Loans/Notes				
Other				
Entertainment/Recreation:				
Eating Out				
Trips/Vacations				
Activities				
Babysitters/Child Care				
Other				
Miscellaneous:				
Toiletries/Cosmetics				
Beauty/Barber				
Pets				
Allowances				
Subscriptions				
Gifts/Christmas				
Stamps/Postage				
Other				
TOTAL AMOUNT SPENT:	$			

* = Fixed Expenses
** = Additional policies not included in employment package

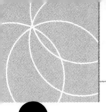

Financial Institutions

CHAPTER 16 • Financial Management

Financial Institutions	
Provider	**Services/Differences**
Commercial Banks	Offer checking, savings, and interest-bearing checking NOW (negotiable order of withdrawal) accounts, lending, credit cards, investments, safe deposit boxes, ATMs, direct deposit, computer or wire transfers, trust services, business services, truncation (retains the checks and forwards a bank statement); are insured by the FDIC's (Federal Deposit Insurance Corporation) Bank Insurance Fund
Savings and Loan Associations	Are similar to commercial banks now that both offer interest-bearing checking NOW accounts; specialize in home mortgage loans; have *FSB* (Federal Savings Bank) or the word *savings* in their title; are insured by the FDIC's Savings Association Insurance Fund
Mutual Savings Banks	Are depositor-owned savings and loan companies; offer interest-bearing NOW accounts and consumer loans; are insured by the state or the FDIC
Credit Unions	Have limited customer base (members with a common bond [work, church, union, occupation]); run the business of lending and investing funds; are insured by the National Credit Union Share Insurance Fund (NCUSIF)
Stock Brokerage Firms	Buy and sell securities; offer cash management accounts (combines checking, borrowing, and security buying with automatic account management); are not federally insured but may be privately insured
Insurance Companies	Sell policies to protect against risks; offer tax shelters, annuities, and retirement plans; may offer combined help with cash management, investments, and insurance
Consumer Banks	Offer services for individuals only (no business accounts); offer savings but not checking services; are not federally insured but may be privately insured

Liquid Assets

CHAPTER 16 • Financial Management

Liquid Assets	
Assets are items owned that have value (clothes, a car, electronic equipment, art, jewels, a house, etc.). Liquidity is the ease with which you can transfer an asset into cash. Liquid assets (also known as monetary assets) are items that can be easily changed into cash without losing value. Although assets have value, they may not have liquidity.	
Liquid Asset	**Definition**
Cash	Money in the form of currency
Checking Accounts	Funds held by a financial institution available to the client on demand
NOW Accounts	Negotiable order of withdrawal accounts; usually requiring a minimum deposit and providing interest-earning checking
Super NOW Accounts	Also referred to as Checking Plus; accounts requiring a large minimum balance but providing substantial interest for the checking account
Savings Accounts	Also called passbook accounts; accounts providing a no-risk investment with no minimum balances but no check-writing privileges
Money Market Deposit Accounts (MMDAs)	Government-insured savings accounts that provide high interest (at money market rates) but have limited check-writing privileges
Money Market Mutual Funds (MMMFs)	A non-insured pooling of thousands of investors' resources to invest in relatively safe and high-return securities (T-Bills) and corporations
Certificates of Deposit (CDs)	A savings account in which assets are frozen (not accessible) for a period of time (which may vary from one week to one year or longer with severe penalties for early withdrawals) and in which interest rates are also locked (or set)
U.S. Treasury Bill (T-Bill)	A short-term (three-month, six-month, and one-year maturities) government security with $10,000 as the smallest denomination of investment
U.S. Series EE Savings Bonds	A short-term investment (for at least five years) in which one purchases the bond for 50% of its face value and can redeem it upon maturity (after twenty years) for the full face value
U.S. Series HH Savings Bonds	Treasury-issued bonds paying a fixed semiannual interest; can be purchased only with EE bonds

Personal Inventory

CHAPTER 17 • Jobs and Income

Identify your assets, talents, skills, and experiences. You may find several things you can do, have done, or can develop the ability to do. List your assets. You may underline or highlight any of the suggested ideas that apply to you. Do the same with your talents, skills you have obtained, and work experience you have acquired.

Personal Assets	Talents	Skills Developed	Work Experience
Health	Coordination	Sports	Coaching
Self-motivation	Singing voice	Singing	Singing solos at weddings
Intelligence	Analysis	Astronomy	VBS teaching
Patience	Artistry	Painting	Working in a nursery
Compassion	Creativity	Cooking	Babysitting
Humor	Public speech	Debating	Typing
Organization	Endurance	Hiking	Being a trail guide

Evaluation

Answer the following on a separate sheet of paper.

1. Do any of your interests, pastimes, or hobbies coincide with your talents and skills?

2. In which ways have you developed or can you develop and use your abilities and talents?

3. Do any of your work experiences build on your physical assets? Your talents? Your skills?

4. In which activities and experiences have you enjoyed using your talents and skills the most?

5. Do you wish to expand any previous experiences into a career?

6. Which personal asset would you like most to use in a career?

Career Search

CHAPTER 17 • Jobs and Income

Search

1. Choose a specific career to research.

2. Using directories, periodicals, and other publications in your library, find out more about this career. Many of the materials you need may be found in the reference section. Answer the following questions:
   a) What educational background is needed?
   b) What experience credentials should be included?
   c) What personal traits are preferable for this career?
   d) What are the job duties and responsibilities?
   e) What are the typical working conditions?

3. Interview someone in this career. Ask these questions:
   a) How was he led toward this career?
   b) How did he prepare for this work?
   c) What does he like the most about his job?
   d) How does his occupation benefit him personally?
   e) What advice would he give to anyone interested in this type of work?

4. Draw a possible career ladder for this career.

5. Assess your personal assets, talents, and skills that would be useful in this career.

6. Identify several employers who would hire someone for this type of work.

7. Write a sample letter to one of these employers, asking for a specific position in the company.

8. List questions to ask this employer in the job interview.

Compile

1. Assemble all this information in the order presented above.

2. Create a title page that includes the career name, your name, the class, and the date.

3. Place the information neatly in a binder or folder.

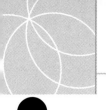

Resumé Tips

CHAPTER 17 • Jobs and Income

Things to Remember

- Resumés must be well organized and brief. Employers spend about twenty seconds reviewing a resumé.
- Resumés should be arranged in the order that best emphasizes one's assets as well as the job prerequisites.
- The outline should be parallel, grammatically correct, without errors, and styled well (font and form).
- Resumés should be reproduced with quality ink and paper.
- Hand the resumé to the employer in person or send it with a cover letter to introduce yourself.

Example Outline

Name

Address

Telephone number (home and cell phone)

Career Objective

Brief description of the type of position you wish to be considered for. If you are unwilling to relocate, your geographic preference may be indicated in this section. (Sometimes it is better to state specific location preferences in a job interview.)

Experience

This section may discuss full- and part-time work experience, summer jobs, volunteer experiences, extended research and study projects, and graduate assistantships. List position, title, and description of duties, tasks performed, responsibilities, etc. If you have military experience, list the branch of service, dates, type of discharge, rank at time of discharge, and areas of responsibility. Keep everything easy to read, bulleted, and in outline form.

Education (may list prior to experience if it is a stronger asset)

Name of high school, college or university, dates attended, degrees received, major field, and grade point average on a 4.0 scale. List significant information about related courses, academic honors, field experiences, and special skills (language proficiency, etc.). Indicate the percentage of your education you paid for yourself.

Optional Additional Information

If there is plenty of room left on the resumé, you may list here any other assets, skills, or experiences significant to your career objective that are not easily organized or included under another heading. Keep in mind that employers quickly scan resumés and desire only brief and pertinent information.

References

May be listed here or on a separate sheet of paper. In the case of a separate reference list, one should type the following at the end of the resumé: "Will be furnished upon request." References should include former professors or employers who can evaluate your ability to perform in a particular work situation. Be sure to secure a person's permission before you give his name as a reference. When listing references, include the name, title or position, complete and current address, and telephone number of each person.

Resumé Sample

CHAPTER 17 • Jobs and Income

SHIRLEY LEONG NEWSOM

OBJECTIVE

To enhance experience in dental technology and patient-interaction skills while attending classes to become a dental hygienist.

EXPERIENCE

2002–present Oriental Imports Kingsport, TN
Sales Associate
• Meet daily sales goals of at least $1,000.
• Deal with customers daily.
• Stock and multi-task.
• Organize and set up displays.
• Have been elected sales associate of the month once every year.

2000–2002 Comet Sports Store Kingsport, TN
Sales Associate
• Assisted customers in purchasing exercise equipment.
• Assembled various fitness equipment.
• Operated the cash register.

1999–2000 Commander Assisted Living Kingsport, TN
Waitress
• Waited on the residents during their meals.
• Took dinner to residents who could not make it to dinner.
• Reset the dining room.
• Entertained and kept company with the elderly.

EDUCATION

2003–present Kingsport Technical College Kingsport, TN
• Working on an associate's degree in dental hygiene.
• Currently maintaining a 3.6 grade point average.

1999–2003 Tri-Cities Christian Academy Kingsport, TN
• Obtained high school diploma.
• Graduated with a 3.8 grade point average.

REFERENCES

• LouAnn Neal, R.D.H. Relationship: Family Friend
  322 Shaffer Drive
  Gray, TN 13609
  (614) 244-9453

• Gail E. Edwards Relationship: Associate Manager
  128 E. Center Street
  Kingsport, TN 13607
  (614) 263-4900

• Carolina Young Relationship: Neighbor
  105 Shadow Dr.
  Boones Creek, TN 13687
  (614) 223-9651 Cell phone (614) 222-8888

103 SHADOW DR. • BOONES CREEK, TN 13687 • (614) 223-4659
CELL PHONE (614) 431-6879 • E-MAIL SOCCERGIRL18@NET.COM

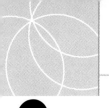

Cover Letter

CHAPTER 17 • Jobs and Income

103 Shadow Drive
Boones Creek, TN 13687
May 21, 2003

Mr. Thomas Businessman
Director of Personnel
Pleasant Dental Services
94-533 Wade Hampton Circle
Kingsport, TN 13604

Dear Mr. Businessman:

Opening paragraph: Briefly introduce yourself and state your purpose in writing. Name the job position or the type of work for which you are applying. Mention how you heard of the opening at this company.

Middle paragraph: Explain why you desire this type of work and why you wish to work for this employer. Mention any previous experience and achievements in this type of work. Refer the employer to an enclosed resumé or other information.

Closing paragraph: Open the door for future contact by asking for an application or interview and indicating how you may be reached. Phrase this request in a courteous manner that will encourage a favorable reply.

Sincerely,

Shirley Leong Newsom

Enclosure

Interview Questions

CHAPTER 17 • Jobs and Income

- **How did you hear about this position?**

- **Why do you want to work for us?**

- **What are your special qualifications for this job?**

- **How will our company benefit if we hire you?**

- **What continuing education programs have you attended in the last year?**

- **What new skills have you developed?**

- **What were your responsibilities in your previous job?**

- **Why did you leave?**

- **If you had an unsatisfied customer, coworker, or student, what would you do?**

- **What is your expected salary?**

- **When would you be available to work?**

- **What are your career goals for the future?**

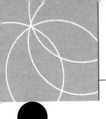

Planned Events

CHAPTER 18 • The Aging Family

Use the following chart to discuss options with your parents. This may prove to be a helpful plan to find out their expectations for the future when you are married or out on your own. Use the shaded rows to add your future spouse's desired occasions and events (be sure to discuss options with his or her parents also). This chart is to provide a basic plan, but it can be changed to suit special needs. It also gives parents an opportunity to discuss and negotiate desires.

Occasions: Include special holidays, birthdays, anniversaries, or vacations (condo or time-share locations)

Traditional Events: Christmas at "home" may also include traditions such as caroling at grandparents', Christmas Eve services, extended family dinner, drive to view Christmas lights and decorations, etc.

Personal Events: These are dates and occasions that you (or your spouse) will want to use for creating your own traditions or events (skiing/boarding trips, personal/family vacations/explorations, etc.).

Dates: Tentative dates (or at least the month) should be placed on the chart with the understanding that dates need to be flexible. Families often rotate between family events that occur at the same time.

Occasion	Traditional Events	Personal Events	Dates
Sample: Christmas	Christmas Eve candlelight service	Soup and sandwiches with friends before	12/24
Sample: Christmas	Family pig-pickin' & gift exchange	Travel to husband's hometown for visit	Weekend before 12/25

Crossword Puzzle

CHAPTER 18 • The Aging Family

Across

1. correct term for Dowager's hump
3. a disease which causes a decrease in height
4. hardening of the arteries
6. _____ generation takes care of the needs of 3 generations
8. shrinking
9. type of retirement that can result in a traumatic experience
10. disease that affects lens transparency
11. Nutrient _____ is most important in the elderly diet.
15. _____ (between 40–65)
16. age of a person, considering his health

Down

2. inflamed joints
5. group of diseases damaging the optic nerve
7. science of studying various effects of old age
11. decline in memory due to changes in the brain
12. blockage of a blood vessel
13. maximum number of years, which has not increased
14. parent-child relationships

Crossword Puzzle, cont.
CHAPTER 18 • The Aging Family

arteriosclerosis
atrophy
cataracts
dementia
density
filial

forced
gerontology
glaucoma
kyphosis
life span
middle age

osteoarthritis
osteoporosis
physical
sandwich
thrombosis